· SERMONS ON ·
THE HOLY SPIRIT

Books of Sermons by Charles Spurgeon
from Hendrickson Publishers

Sermons on the Lord's Supper
Sermons on the Passion of Christ
Sermons on Women of the Old Testament
Sermons on Men of the Old Testament
Sermons about Christmas
Sermons on the Prayers of Christ
Sermons on Cries from the Cross
Sermons on the Resurrection
Sermons on the Love of Christ
Sermons on the Holy Spirit
Sermons on Prayer
Sermons on Great Prayers of the Bible
Sermons on the Second Coming of Christ
Sermons on Heaven and Hell
Sermons on Women of the New Testament
Sermons on Men of the New Testament

· SERMONS ON ·
THE HOLY SPIRIT

HENDRICKSON
PUBLISHERS

Sermons on the Holy Spirit

© 2015 by Hendrickson Publishers, LLC

Published by Hendrickson Publishers
an imprint of Hendrickson Publishing Group
P. O. Box 3473
Peabody, Massachusetts 01961-3473
www.hendricksonpublishinggroup.com

ISBN 978-1-61970-629-3

All rights reserved. No part of this book may be reproduced or transmitted in any form or by any means, electronic or mechanical, including photocopying, recording, or by any information storage and retrieval system, without permission in writing from the publisher.

Originally published by Hendrickson Publishers in *Spurgeon's Sermons on Jesus and the Holy Spirit*.

Printed in the United States of America

Cover photo of Charles Haddon (C. H.) Spurgeon by Herbert Rose Barraud is used by permission of the University of Minnesota Libraries, Special Collections and Rare Books.

Contents

Preface	vii
The Comforter	1
The Power of the Holy Ghost	13
The Holy Ghost, the Great Teacher	27
The Outpouring of the Holy Spirit	41
The Holy Spirit Compared to the Wind	53
The Withering Work of the Spirit	67
The Pentecostal Wind and Fire	81
The Indwelling and Outflowing of the Holy Spirit	95
The Abiding of the Spirit Is the Glory of the Church	109
The Covenant Promise of the Spirit	123
Honey in the Mouth!	137
Index to Key Scriptures	150

In memory of Patricia Klein (1949–2014), our colleague and friend, who spent her life caring for words and who edited this series. She is truly missed.

Preface

Charles Haddon Spurgeon
1834–1892

Ask most people today who Charles Haddon Spurgeon was, and you might be surprised at the answers. Most know he was a preacher, others remember that he was Baptist, and others go so far as to remember that he lived in England during the nineteenth century. All of this is true, yet Charles Haddon Spurgeon was so much more.

Born into a family of Congregationalists in 1834, Spurgeon's father and grandfather were both Independent preachers. These designations seem benign today, but in the mid-nineteenth century, they describe a family committed to a Nonconformist path—meaning they did not conform to the established Church of England. Spurgeon grew up in a rural village, a village virtually cut off from the Industrial Revolution rolling over most of England.

Spurgeon became a Christian at a Primitive Methodist meeting in 1850 at age sixteen. He soon became a Baptist (to the sorrow of his mother) and almost immediately began to preach. Considered a preaching prodigy—"a boy wonder of the fens"—Spurgeon attracted huge audiences and garnered a reputation that reached throughout the countryside and into London. As a result of his great success, Spurgeon was invited to preach at the New Park Street Chapel in London in 1854, when he was just nineteen. When he first preached at the church, they were unable to fill even two hundred seats. Within the year, Spurgeon filled the twelve-hundred-seat church to overflowing. He soon began preaching in larger and larger venues, outgrowing each, until finally in 1861 the Metropolitan Tabernacle was completed, which seated six thousand persons. This would be Spurgeon's home base for the rest of his career, until his death in 1892 at age fifty-seven.

Spurgeon married Susannah Thompson in 1856 and soon they had twin sons, Charles and Thomas, who would later follow him in his work. Spurgeon opened Pastors' College, a training school for preachers, which trained over nine hundred preachers during his lifetime. He also opened orphanages for underprivileged boys and girls, providing education to each of the orphans. And with Susannah, he developed a program to publish and distribute Christian literature. He is said to have preached to over ten million people in his forty years of ministry. His sermons sold over twenty-five thousand copies each week and were translated into twenty languages. He was utterly committed to spreading the gospel through preaching and through the written word.

During Spurgeon's lifetime, the Industrial Revolution transformed England from a rural, agricultural society to an urban, industrial society, with all the attendant difficulties and horrors of a society in major transition. The people displaced by these sweeping changes—factory workers and shopkeepers—became Spurgeon's congregation. From a small village himself and transplanted to a large and inhospitable city, he was a common man and understood innately the spiritual needs of the common people. He was a communicator who made the gospel so relevant, who spoke so brilliantly to people's deepest needs, that listeners welcomed his message.

Keep in mind that Spurgeon preached in the days before microphones or speakers; in other words, he preached without benefit of amplifier systems. Once he preached to a crowd of over twenty-three thousand people without mechanical amplification of any sort. He himself was the electrifying presence on the platform: he did not stand and simply read a stilted sermon. Spurgeon used an outline, developing his themes extemporaneously, and speaking "in common language to common people." His sermons were filled with stories and poetry, drama and emotion. He was larger than life, always in motion, striding back and forth across the stage. He gestured broadly, acted out stories, used humor, and painted word pictures. For Spurgeon, preaching was about communicating the truth of God, and he would use any gift at his disposal to accomplish this.

Spurgeon's preaching was anchored in his spiritual life, a life rich in prayer and the study of Scripture. He was not tempted by fashion, be it theological, social, or political. Scripture was the cornerstone of Spurgeon's life and his preaching. He was an expositional preacher mostly, exploring a passage of Scripture for its meaning both within the text as well as in the lives of each member of his congregation. To Spurgeon, Scripture was alive and specifically relevant to people's lives, whatever their social status, economic situation, or time in which they lived.

One has a sense that Spurgeon embraced God's revelation completely: God's revelation through Jesus Christ, through Scripture, and through his own prayer and study. For him, revelation was not a finished act: God still reveals himself, if one made oneself available. Some recognize Spurgeon for the mystic he was, one who was willing and eager to explore the mysteries of God, able to live with those bits of truth that do not conform to a particular system of theology, perfectly comfortable with saying, "This I know, and this I don't know—yet will I trust."

Each of the sermons in this collection was preached at a different time in Spurgeon's career and each has distinct characteristics. These sermons are not a series, as they were not created or intended to be sequential, nor have they been homogenized or edited to sound as though they are all of a kind. Instead, they reflect the preacher himself, allowing the voice of this remarkable man to ring clearly as he guides the reader into a particular account, a particular event—to experience, with Spurgeon, God's particular revelation.

As you read, *listen*. These words were meant to be heard, not merely read. Listen carefully and you will hear the cadences of this remarkable preaching, the echoes of God's timeless truth traveling across the years. And above all, enjoy Spurgeon's enthusiasm, his fire, his devotion, his zeal to recognize and respond to God's timeless invitation to engage the Creator himself.

The Comforter

Delivered on Sabbath evening, January 21, 1855, at New Park Street Chapel, Southwark. No. 5.

But the Comforter, which is the Holy Ghost, whom the Father will send in my name, he shall teach you all things, and bring all things to your remembrance, whatsoever I have said unto you.—John 14:26

Good old Simeon called Jesus the consolation of Israel; and so he was. Before his actual appearance, his name was the Day-Star—cheering the darkness, and prophetic of the rising sun. To him they looked with the same hope which cheers the nightly watcher, when, from the lonely castle-top, he sees the fairest of the stars, and hails her as the usher of the morn. When He was on earth, he must have been the consolation of all those who were privileged to be his companions. We can imagine how readily the disciples would run to Christ to tell him of their griefs, and how sweetly with that matchless intonation of his voice, he would speak to them and bid their fears be gone. Like children, they would consider him as their Father; and to him every want, every groan, every sorrow, every agony would at once be carried, and he, like a wise physician, had a balm for every wound; he had mingled a cordial for their every care; and readily did he dispense some mighty remedy to allay all the fever of their troubles. Oh! it must have been sweet to have lived with Christ. Surely sorrows then were but joys in masks because they gave an opportunity to go to Jesus to have them removed. Oh! would to God, some of us may say, that we could have lain our weary heads upon the bosom of Jesus, and that our birth had been in that happy era, when we might have heard his kind voice, and seen his kind look, when he said "Let the weary ones come unto me."

But now he was about to die. Great prophecies were to be fulfilled, and great purposes were to be answered; and therefore Jesus must go. It behooved him to suffer, that he might be made a propitiation for our sins. It behooved him to slumber in the dust awhile, that he might perfume the chamber of the grave, to make it

> No more a charnel house to fence
> The relics of lost innocence.

It behooved him to have a resurrection, that we, who shall one day be the dead in Christ, might [at the Second Coming] rise first, and in glorious bodies stand upon earth. And it behooved him that he should ascend up on high, that he might lead captivity captive; that he might chain the fiends of Hell; that he might lash them to his chariot wheels and drag them up high Heaven's hill, to make them feel a second overthrow from his right arm when he should dash them from the pinnacles of Heaven down to deeper depths beneath. "It is right I should go away from you," said Jesus, "for if I go not away, the Comforter will not come." Jesus must go. Weep ye disciples. Jesus must be gone. Mourn ye poor ones who are to be left without a Comforter. But hear how kindly Jesus speaks: "I will not leave you comfortless: I will pray the Father, and he shall send you another Comforter, who shall be with you, and shall dwell in you forever." He would not leave those few poor sheep alone in the wilderness; he would not desert his children and leave them fatherless. Albeit that he had a mighty mission which did fill his heart and hand; albeit that he had so much to perform that we might have thought that even *his* gigantic intellect would be overburdened. Albeit he had so much to suffer that we might suppose his whole soul to be concentrated upon the thought of the sufferings to be endured—yet it was not so; before he left, he gave soothing words of comfort; like the good Samaritan, he poured in oil and wine; and we see what he promised: "I will send you another Comforter—one who shall be just what I have been, yea even more; who shall console you in your sorrows, remove your doubts, comfort you in your afflictions, and stand as my vicar on earth, to do that which I would have done, had I tarried with you."

Before I discourse of the Holy Ghost as the Comforter, I must make one or two remarks on the different translations of the word rendered "Comforter." The Flemish translation, which you are aware is adopted by Roman Catholics, has left the word untranslated, and gives it "Paraclete." "But the Paraclete, which is the Holy Ghost, whom the Father will send in my name, he shall teach you all things." This is the original Greek word, and it has some other meanings besides "Comforter." Sometimes it means the monitor or instructor: "I will send you another monitor, another teacher." Frequently it means "advocate;" but the most common meaning of the word is that which we have here: "I will send you another *Comforter*." However, we cannot pass over those other two interpretations without saying something upon them.

"I will send you another *teacher*." Jesus Christ had been the official teacher for his saints whilst on earth. They called no man Rabbi except Christ. They sat at no men's feet to learn their doctrines; but they had them direct from the lips of him who "spake as never man spake." "And now," says he,

> ... when I am gone, where shall you find the great infallible teacher? Shall I set you up a Pope at Rome, to whom you shall go, and who shall be your infallible oracle? Shall I give you the councils of the church to be held to decide all knotty points?

Christ said no such thing.

> I am the infallible paraclete or teacher, and when I am gone, I will send you another teacher, and he shall be the person who is to explain Scripture; he shall be the authoritative oracle of God, who shall make all dark things light, who shall unravel mysteries, who shall untwist all knots of revelation, and shall make you understand what you could not discover, had it not been for his influence.

And beloved, no man ever learns anything aright, unless he is taught of the Spirit. You may learn election [to salvation], and you may know it so that you shall be damned by it, if you are not taught of the Holy Ghost; for I have known some who have learned election to their soul's destruction; they have learned it, so that they said they were of the elect, whereas they had no marks, no evidences, and no work of the Holy Ghost in their souls. There is a way of learning truth in Satan's college, and holding it in licentiousness; but if so, it shall be to your souls as poison to your veins, and prove your everlasting ruin. No man can know Jesus Christ unless he is taught of God. There is no doctrine of the Bible which can be safely, thoroughly, and truly learned, except by the agency of the one authoritative teacher. Ah! tell me not of systems of divinity, tell me not of schemes of theology; tell me not of infallible commentators, or most learned and most arrogant doctors; but tell me of the Great Teacher, who shall instruct us, the sons of God, and shall make us wise to understand all things. He is *the* Teacher; it matters not what this or that man says; I rest on no man's boasting authority, nor will you. Ye are not to be carried away with the craftiness of men, nor sleight of words; this is the authoritative oracle, the Holy Ghost resting in the hearts of his children.

The other translation is *advocate*. Have you ever thought how the Holy Ghost can be said to be an advocate? You know Jesus Christ is called the wonderful, the counselor, and mighty God; but how can the Holy Ghost be said to be an advocate? I suppose it is thus: he is an advocate on earth to plead against the enemies of the cross. How was it that Paul could so ably plead before Felix and Agrippa?[1] How was it that the Apostles stood unawed before the magistrates and confessed their Lord? How has it come to pass that in all times God's ministers have been made fearless as lions, and their brows have been firmer than brass, their hearts sterner than steel, and their words like the language of God? Why, it is simply for this reason, that it was not the man who pleaded, but it was God the Holy Ghost pleading through him. Have you never seen an earnest minister, with hands uplifted and eyes dropping tears, pleading with the sons of men? Have you never admired that portrait from the hand of old John Bunyan? [It shows] a grave person with eyes uplifted to heaven, the best of books in his hand, the law of truth written on his lips, the world behind his back, standing as if he pleaded with men, and a crown of gold hanging over his head. Who gave that minister so blessed a manner and such goodly matter? Whence came his skill? Did he acquire it in the college? Did he learn it in the seminary? Ah! no; he learned it of the God of Jacob; he learned it of the Holy Ghost; for the Holy Ghost is the great counselor who teaches us how to advocate his cause aright.

But, besides this, the Holy Ghost is the advocate in men's hearts. Ah! I have known men reject a doctrine until the Holy Ghost began to illumine them. We who are the advocates of the truth are often very poor pleaders; we spoil our cause by the words we use; but it is a mercy that the brief is in the hand of a special pleader, who will advocate successfully and overcome the sinner's opposition. Did you ever know him fail once? Brethren, I speak to your souls—has not God in old times convinced you of sin? Did not the Holy Ghost come and prove that you were guilty, although no minister could ever get you out of your self-righteousness? Did he not advocate Christ's righteousness? Did he not stand and tell you that your works were filthy rags? And when you had well-nigh still refused to listen to his voice, did he not fetch Hell's drum and make it sound about your ears, bidding you look through the vista of future years and see the throne set, and the books open, and the sword brandished, and Hell burning, and fiends howling, and the damned shrieking forever? And did he not thus convince you of the judgment to come? He is a mighty advocate when he pleads in the soul of sin, of righteousness, and of the judgment to come. Blessed advocate! Plead in my heart, plead with my conscience. When I sin, make conscience bold to tell me of it; when I err, make conscience speak at once; and when I turn aside to crooked ways, then advocate the cause of righteousness, and bid me sit down in confusion, knowing my guiltiness in the sight of God.

But there is yet another sense in which the Holy Ghost advocates, and that is, he advocates our cause with Jesus Christ, with groanings that cannot be uttered. O my soul, thou art ready to burst within me! O my heart, thou art swelled with grief;

---

[1] Felix and Agrippa: rulers before whom Paul was able to witness about Jesus.

the hot tide of my emotion would well-nigh overflow the channels of my veins. I long to speak, but the very desire chains my tongue. I wish to pray, but the fervency of my feeling curbs my language. There is a groaning within that cannot be uttered. Do you know who can utter that groaning, who can understand it, and who can put it into heavenly language and utter it in a celestial tongue, so that Christ can hear it? Oh! yes; it is God the Holy Spirit; he advocates our cause with Christ, and then Christ advocates it with his Father. He is the advocate, who maketh intercession for us, with groanings that cannot be uttered.

Having thus explained the Spirit's office as teacher and advocate, we come now to the translation of our version—the *Comforter;* and here I shall have three divisions. First, the *comforter;* secondly, the *comfort;* and thirdly, the *comforted.*

I. First, then, the *Comforter.*

Briefly let me run over in my mind, and in your minds too, the characteristics of this glorious Comforter. Let me tell you some of the attributes of his comfort, so that you may understand how well adapted he is to your case.

And first, we will remark that God the Holy Ghost is a very *loving* Comforter. I am in distress and want consolation. Some passer-by hears of my sorrow, and he steps within, sits down and essays [attempts] to cheer me; he speaks soothing words—but he loves me not, he is a stranger, he knows me not at all, he has only come in to try his skill—and what is the consequence? His words run over me like oil upon a slab of marble—they are like the pattering rain upon the rock; they do not break my grief; it stands unmoved as adamant, because he has no love for me. But let someone who loves me dearly as his own life come and plead with me, then truly his words are music; they taste like honey; he knows the password of the doors of my heart, and my ear is attentive to every word, I catch the intonation of each syllable as it falls, for it is like the harmony of the harps of Heaven. Oh! there is a voice in love, it speaks a language which is its own—it is a idiom and an accent which none can mimic; wisdom cannot imitate it, oratory cannot attain unto it; it is love alone which can reach the mourning heart; love is the only handkerchief which can wipe the mourner's tears away. And is not the Holy Ghost a loving Comforter? Dost thou know, O saint, how much the Holy Spirit loves thee? Canst thou measure the love of the Spirit? Dost thou know how great is the affection of his soul towards thee? Go, measure Heaven with thy span; go, weigh the mountains in the scales; go, take the ocean's water, and tell [number] each drop; go count the sand upon the sea's wide shore, and when thou hast accomplished this, thou canst tell how much he loveth thee. He has loved thee long, he has loved thee well; he loved thee ever, and he still shall love thee. Surely he is the person to comfort thee, because he loves. Admit him, then, to your heart, O Christian, that he may comfort you in your distress.

But next he is a *faithful* Comforter. Love sometimes proves unfaithful. "Oh! sharper than a serpent's tooth"[2] is an unfaithful friend! Oh! far more bitter than the gall of bitterness, to have a friend to turn from me in my distress! Oh! woe of woes, to have one who loves me in my prosperity forsake me in the dark day of my trouble. Sad indeed—but such is not God's Spirit. He ever loves, and loves even to the end—a faithful Comforter. Child of God, you are in trouble. A little while ago you found him a sweet and loving Comforter; you obtained relief from him when others were but broken cisterns; he sheltered you in his bosom, and carried you in his arms. Oh, wherefore dost thou distrust him now? Away with thy fears! For he is a faithful Comforter. "Ah! but "thou sayest, "I fear I shall be sick and shall be deprived of his ordinances." Nevertheless, he shall visit thee on thy sick bed, and sit by thy side to give the consolation. "Ah! but I have distresses greater than you can conceive of, wave upon wave rolleth over me; deep calleth unto deep at the noise of the Eternal's waterspouts." Nevertheless, he will be faithful to his promise. "Ah! but I have sinned." So thou hast, but sin cannot sever thee from his love; he loves thee still. Think not, O poor downcast child of God, because the scars of thine old sins have marred thy beauty, that he loves thee less because of that blemish. Oh, no! He loved thee when he foreknew thy sin; he loved thee with the knowledge of what the aggregate of thy wickedness would be; and he does not love the less now. Come to him in all boldness of faith; tell him thou hast grieved him, and he will forget thy wandering, and will receive thee again; the kisses of his love shall be bestowed upon thee, and the arms of his grace shall embrace thee. He is faithful: trust him—he will never deceive you; trust him—he will never leave you.

Again, he is an *unwearied* Comforter. I have sometimes tried to comfort persons that have been tried. You now and then meet with the case of a nervous person. You ask, "What is your trouble?" You are told, and you essay, if possible, to remove it, but while you are preparing your artillery to batter the trouble, you find that it has shifted its quarters, and is occupying quite a different position. You change your argument and begin again; but lo, it is again gone, and you are bewildered. You feel like Hercules cutting off the ever-growing heads of the Hydra, and you give up your task in despair. You meet with persons whom it is impossible to comfort, reminding me of the man who locked himself up in fetters and threw the key away, so that nobody could unlock him. I have found some in the fetters of despair. "O, I am the man," say they, "that has seen affliction; pity me, pity me, O my friends;" and the more you try to comfort such people, the worse they get; and therefore, out of all heart [discouraged], we leave them to wander alone among the tombs of their former joys. But the Holy Ghost is never out of heart with those whom he wishes to comfort. He attempts to comfort us and we run away from the

---

[2] The full quote, from Shakespeare's "King Lear," is: "How sharper than a serpent's tooth it is; To have a thankless child!"

sweet cordial; he gives some sweet draught to cure us, and we will not drink it; he gives some wondrous potion to charm away all our troubles, and we put it away from us. Still he pursues us; and though we say that we will not be comforted, he says we *shall* be, and when he has said, he does it—he is not to be wearied by all our sins, not by all our murmurings.

And oh, how *wise* a Comforter is the Holy Ghost. Job had comforters, and I think he spoke the truth when he said, "Miserable comforters are ye all." But I dare say they esteemed themselves wise; and when the young man Elihu rose to speak, they thought he had a world of impudence. Were they not "grave and reverend seniors?" Did not they comprehend his grief and sorrow? If they could not comfort him, who could? But they did not find out the cause. They thought he was not really a child of God, that he was self-righteous; and they have him the wrong physic. It is a bad case when the doctor mistakes the disease and gives a wrong prescription, and so, perhaps, kills the patient. Sometimes, when we go and visit people, we mistake their disease— we want to comfort them on this point, whereas they do not require any such comfort at all, and they would be better left alone than spoiled by such unwise comforters as we are. But oh! How wise the Holy Spirit is! He takes the soul, lays it on the table, and dissects it in a moment; he finds out the root of the matter, he sees where the complaint is, and then he applies the knife where something is required to be taken away, or puts a plaster where the sore is; and he never mistakes. Oh! how wise, the blessed Holy Ghost! From every comforter, I turn and leave them all, for thou art he who alone givest the wisest consolation.

Then mark how *safe* a Comforter the Holy Ghost is. All comfort is not safe; mark that. There is a young man over there very melancholy. You know how he became so. He stepped into the house of God and heard a powerful preacher, and the word was blessed and convinced him of sin. When he went home, his father and the rest found there was something different about him, "Oh," they said, "John is mad; he is crazy," and what said his mother? "Send him into the country for a week, let him go to the ball or to the theater." John! Did you find any comfort there? "Ah no; they made me worse, for while I was there, I thought Hell might open and swallow me up." Did you find any relief in the gaieties of the world? "No," say you, "I thought it was [an] idle waste of time." Alas! this is miserable comfort, but it is the comfort of the worldling; and when a Christian gets into distress, how many will recommend him this remedy and the other. "Go and hear Mr. So-and-so preach; have a few friends at your house; read such-and-such a consoling volume;" and very likely it is the most unsafe advice in the world. The devil will sometimes come to men's souls as a false comforter, and he will say to the soul, "What need is there to make all this ado about repentance? You are no worse than other people," and he will try to make the soul believe that what is [actually] presumption is the real assurance of the Holy Ghost; thus he deceives many by false comfort. Ah, there have been many, like infants, destroyed by elixirs given to lull them to sleep; many have been ruined by the cry of "peace, peace," when there is no peace, hearing gentle things when they ought to be stirred to the quick. Cleopatra's asp was brought in a basket of flowers; and men's ruin often lurks in fair and sweet speeches. But the Holy Ghost's comfort is safe, and you may rest on it. Let him speak the word, and there is a reality about it; let him give the cup of consolation, and you may drink it to the bottom, for in its depths there are no dregs, nothing to intoxicate or ruin—it is all safe.

Moreover, the Holy Ghost is an *active* Comforter: he does not comfort by words, but by deeds. Some comfort by [saying,] "Be ye warmed and be ye filled"—giving nothing. But the Holy Ghost gives, he intercedes with Jesus; he gives us promises, he gives us grace, and so he comforts us. Mark again, he is always a *successful* Comforter; he never attempts what he cannot accomplish.

Then to close up, he is an *ever-present* Comforter, so that you never have to send for him. Your God is always near you, and when you need comfort in your distress, behold, the word is nigh thee, it is in thy mouth, and in thy heart; he is an ever-present help in time of trouble. I wish I had time to expand these thoughts; but I cannot.

II. The second thing is the *comfort*.

Now there are some persons who make a great mistake about the influence of the Holy Spirit. A foolish man who had [a] fancy to preach in a certain pulpit—though in truth he was quite incapable of the duty—called upon the minister, and assured him solemnly that it had been revealed to him by the Holy Ghost, that he was to preach in his pulpit. "Very well," said the minister, "I suppose I must not doubt your assertion, but as it has not been revealed to me that I am to let you preach, you must go your way until it is." I have heard many fanatical persons say the Holy Spirit revealed this and that to them. Now that is very generally revealed [eventually, to be] nonsense. The Holy Ghost does not reveal anything fresh now. He brings old things to our remembrance. "He shall teach you all things, and bring all things to your remembrance, whatsoever I have told you." The canon of revelation is closed; there is no more to be added. God does not give a fresh revelation, but he rivets the old one. When it has been forgotten, and laid in the dusty chamber of our memory, he fetches it out and cleans the picture, but does not paint a new one. There are no new doctrines, but the old ones are often revived. It is not, I say, by any new revelation that the Spirit comforts. He does so by telling us old things over again; he brings a fresh lamp to manifest the treasures hidden in Scripture; he unlocks the strong chests in which the truth had long lain, and he points to secret chambers filled with untold riches; but he coins no more, for enough is done. Believer! there is enough in the Bible for thee to live upon forever. If thou shouldst outnumber the years of Methusaleh, there would be no need for a fresh revelation; if thou shouldst live till Christ should come upon the earth, there would be no necessity for the addition of a single word; if thou shouldst go down as deep as Jonah, or even descend as David said he did, into the belly of Hell, still there would be enough in the Bible to comfort thee without a supplementary sentence. But Christ says, "He shall take of mine and shall show it unto you." Now let me just tell you briefly what it is the Holy Ghost tells us.

Ah! does he not whisper to the heart,

> Saint, be of good cheer; there is one who died for thee; look to Calvary; behold his wounds; see the torrent gushing from his side; there is thy purchaser, and thou art secure. He loves thee with an everlasting love, and this chastisement is meant for thy good; each stroke is working thy healing; by the blueness of the wound, thy soul is made better. "Whom he loveth he chasteneth, and scourgeth every son whom he receiveth." Doubt not his grace, because of thy tribulation, but believe that he loveth thee as much in seasons of trouble as in times of happiness.

And then, moreover, he says, "What is all thy suffering compared with that of thy Lord's, or what, when weighed in the scales of Jesu's agonies, is all thy distress?" And especially at times does the Holy Ghost take back the veil of heaven, and lets the soul behold the glory of the upper world! Then it is that the saint can say, "Oh, thou art a Comforter to me!"

> *Let cares like a wild deluge come,*
> *And storms of sorrow fall;*
> *May I but safely reach my home,*
> *My God, my heaven, my all.*

Some of you could follow, were I to tell of manifestations of heaven. You too have left sun, moon, and stars, at your feet, while in your flight, outstripping the tardy lightning, you have seemed to enter the gates of pearl, and tread the golden streets, borne aloft on wings of the Spirit. But here we must not trust ourselves, lest, lost in reverie, we forget our theme.

III. And now thirdly, who are the *comforted* persons!

I like, you know, at the end of my sermon to cry out "Divide! Divide!" There are two parties here—some who are the comforted, and others who are the comfortless ones—some who have received the consolation of the Holy Ghost, and some who have not. Now let us try and sift you, and see which is the chaff; and which is the wheat; and may God grant that some of the chaff may this night be transformed into his wheat.

You may say, "How am I to know whether I am a recipient of the comfort of the Holy Ghost?" You may know it by one rule. If you have received one blessing from

God, you will receive all other blessings too. Let me explain myself. If I could come here as an auctioneer, and sell the gospel off in lots, I should dispose of it all. If I could say, "Here is justification through the blood of Christ, free, given away, gratis;" many a one would say, "I will have justification: give it me; I wish to be justified, I wish to be pardoned." Suppose I took sanctification, the giving up of all sin, a thorough change of heart, leaving off drunkenness and swearing. Many would say,

> I don't want *that*; I should like to go to Heaven, but I do not want that holiness; I should like to be saved at last, but I should like to have my drink still; I should like to enter glory, but then I must have an oath or two on the road.

Nay, but sinner, if thou hast one blessing, thou shalt have *all*. God will never divide the gospel. He will not give justification to that man, and sanctification to another; pardon to one and holiness to another. No, it all goes together. Whom he calls, them he justifies; whom he justifies, them he sanctifies; and whom he sanctifies, them he also glorifies. Oh; if I could lay down nothing but the *comforts* of the gospel, ye would fly to them as flies do to honey. When ye come to be ill, ye send for the clergyman. Ah! you all want your minister then to come and give you consoling words. But if he be an honest man, he will not give some of you a particle of consolation. He will not commence pouring oil, when the knife would be better. I want to make a man feel his sins before I dare tell him anything about Christ. I want to probe into his soul and make him feel that he is lost before I tell him anything about the purchased blessing. It is the ruin of many to tell them, "Now just believe on Christ, and that is all you have to do." If, instead of dying, they get better, they rise up whitewashed hypocrites—that is all. I have heard of a city missionary who kept a record of two thousand persons who were supposed to be on their death-bed, but recovered, and whom he should have put down as converted persons had they died, and how many do you think lived a Christian life afterwards, out of the two-thousand! Not two! Positively he could only find one who was found to live afterwards in the fear of God. Is it not horrible that when men and women come to die, they should cry, "Comfort, comfort?" and that hence their friends conclude that they are children of God, while, after all, they have no right to consolation, but are intruders upon the enclosed grounds of the blessed God. Oh God! May these people ever be kept from having comfort when they have no right to it! Have you the other blessings? Have you had conviction of sin? Have you ever felt your guilt before God? Have your souls been humbled at Jesus' feet? And have you been made to look to Calvary alone for your refuge? If not, you have no right to consolation. Do not take an atom of it. The Spirit is a Convincer before he is a Comforter; and you must have the other operations of the Holy Spirit before you can derive anything from this.

And now I have done. You have heard what this babbler hath said once more. What has it been? Something about the Comforter. But let me ask you, before you go—what do you know about the Comforter? Each one of you, before descending the steps of this chapel, let this solemn question thrill through your souls: "What do you know of the Comforter?" Oh! poor souls, if ye know not the Comforter, I will tell you what you shall know—you shall know the Judge! If ye know not the Comforter on earth, ye shall know the Condemner in the next world, who shall cry, "Depart, ye cursed, into everlasting fire in Hell." Well might [George] Whitfield call out, "O earth, earth, earth, hear the Word of the Lord!" If we were to live here forever, ye might slight the gospel; if ye had a lease of your lives, ye might despise the Comforter. But sirs, ye must die. Since last we met together, probably some have gone to their long last home; and ere we meet again in this sanctuary, some here will be amongst the glorified above, or amongst the damned below. Which will it be? Let your soul answer. If tonight you fell down dead in your pews, or where you are standing in the gallery, where would you be? In *Heaven* or in *Hell*?

Ah! deceive not yourselves; let conscience have its perfect work; and if, in the sight of God, you are obliged to say, "I tremble and fear lest my portion should be with unbelievers," listen one moment, and then I have done with thee. "He that believeth and is baptized shall be saved, and he that believeth not shall be damned." Weary sinner, hellish sinner, thou who art the Devil's castaway, reprobate, profligate, harlot, robber, thief, adulterer, fornicator, drunkard, swearer, Sabbath-breaker! I speak to thee as well as the rest. I exempt no man. God hath said there is no exemption here. "*Whosoever* believeth in the name of Jesus Christ shall be saved." Sin is no barrier: thy guilt is no obstacle. Whosoever—though he were as black as Satan, though he were filthy as a fiend—whosoever this night believes, shall have every sin forgiven, shall have every crime effaced, shall have every iniquity blotted out; shall be saved in the Lord Jesus Christ, and shall stand in Heaven safe and secure. That is the glorious gospel. God apply it home to your hearts, and give you faith in Jesus!

> *We have listened to the preacher—*
> *Truth by him has now been shown;*
> *But we want a greater teacher,*
> *From the everlasting throne:*
> *Application is the work of God alone.*

The Power of the Holy Ghost

Delivered on Sabbath morning, June 17, 1855, at New Park Street Chapel. No. 30.

The power of the Holy Ghost.—Romans 15:13

Power is the special and peculiar prerogative of God, and God alone. "Twice have I have heard this: that power belongeth unto God." God is God: and power belongeth to him. If he delegates a portion of it to his creatures, yet still it is *his* power. The sun, although he is "like a bridegroom coming out of his chamber, and rejoiceth as a strong man to run his race," yet has no power to perform his motions except as God directs him. The stars, although they travel in their orbits and none could stay them, yet have neither might nor force except that which God daily infuses into them. The tall archangel, near his throne, who outshines a comet in its blaze, though he is one of those who excel in strength and hearken to the voice of the commands of God, yet has no might except that which his Maker gives to him. As for Leviathan, who so maketh the sea to boil like a pot that one would think the deep were hoary [ancient]: as for Behemoth, who drinketh up Jordan at a draught, and boasteth that he can snuff up rivers; as for those majestic creatures that are found on earth, they owe their strength to him who fashioned their bones of steel and made their sinews of brass. And when we think of man, if he has might or power, it is so small and insignificant, that we can scarcely call it such; yea, when it is at its greatest—when he sways his scepter, when he commands hosts, when he rules nations—still the power belongeth unto God; and it is true, "Twice have I heard this, that power belongeth unto God." This exclusive prerogative of God is to be found in each of the three persons of the glorious Trinity. The Father hath power:

for by his word were the heavens made, and all the host of them, by his strength all things stand, and through him they fulfill their destiny. The Son hath power: for like his Father, he is the Creator of all things; "Without him was not anything made that was made," and "by him all things consist." And the Holy Spirit hath power. It is concerning the power of the Holy Ghost that I shall speak this morning; and may you have a practical exemplification of that attribute in your own hearts, when you shall feel that the influence of the Holy Ghost is being poured out upon me, so that I am speaking the words of the living God to your souls, and bestowed upon you when you are feeling the effects of it in your own spirits.

We shall look at the power of the Holy Ghost in three ways this morning. First, *the outward and visible displays of it,* second, *the inward and spiritual manifestations of it,* and third, *the future and expected works thereof.* The power of the Spirit will thus, I trust, be made clearly present to your souls.

First, then, we are to view the power of the Spirit in the *outward and visible displays of it.*

The power of the Spirit has not been dormant; it has exerted itself. Much has been done by the Spirit of God already; more than could have been accomplished by any being except the Infinite, Eternal, Almighty Jehovah, of whom the Holy Spirit is one person. There are four works which are the outward and manifest signs of the power of the Spirit: creation works; resurrection works; works of attestation or of witness; and works of grace. Of each of the works I shall speak very briefly.

1. First, the Spirit has manifested the omnipotence of his power in *creation works*; for though not very frequently in Scripture, yet sometimes creation is ascribed to the Holy Ghost, as well as to the Father and the Son. The creation of the heavens above us is said to be the work of God's Spirit. This you will see at once by referring to the sacred Scriptures, Job 26:13, "By his Spirit he hath garnished the heavens, his hand hath formed the crooked serpent." All the stars of heaven are said to have been placed aloft by the Spirit, and one particular constellation called the "crooked serpent" is specially pointed out as his handiwork. He looseth the bands of Orion; he bindeth the sweet influences of the Pleiades, and guides Aeturus with his sons. He made all those stars that shine in heaven. The heavens were garnished by his hands, and he formed the crooked serpent by his might. So also in those continued acts of creation which are still performed in the world; as the bringing forth of man and animals, their birth and generation. These are ascribed also to the Holy Ghost. If you look at the 104th Psalm, at the 29th verse, you will read,

> Thou hidest thy face, they are troubled: thou takest away their breath, they die, and return to their dust. Thou sendest forth thy Spirit, they are created and thou renewest the face of the earth.

So that the creation of every man is the work of the Spirit: and the creation of all life and all flesh—existence in this world is as much to be ascribed to the power of the Spirit as the first garnishing of the heavens, or the fashioning of the crooked serpent.

But if you will look in the 1st chapter of Genesis, you will there see more particularly set forth that peculiar operation of power upon the universe which was put forth by the Holy Spirit; you will then discover what was his special work. In the 2nd verse of the 1st chapter of Genesis, we read, "And the earth was without form, and void; and darkness was upon the face of the deep. And the Spirit of God moved upon the face of the waters." We know not how remote the period of the creation of this globe may be—certainly many millions of years before the time of Adam. Our planet has passed through various stages of existence, and different kinds of creatures have lived on its surface, all of which have been fashioned by God. But before that era came, wherein man should be its principal tenant and monarch, the Creator gave up the world to confusion. He allowed the inward fires to burst up from beneath and melt all the solid matter, so that all kinds of substances were commingled in one vast mass of disorder; the only name you could give to the world then was, that it was a chaotic mass of matter; what it should be, you could not guess or define. It was entirely without form, and void, and darkness was upon the face of the deep. The Spirit came, and stretching his broad wings, bade the darkness disperse, and as he moved over it, all the different portions of matter came into their places, and it was no longer "without form, and void"; but became round like its sister planets, and moved, singing the high praises of God—not discordantly as it had done before, but as one great note in the vast scale of creation.

Milton very beautifully describes this work of the Spirit in thus bringing order out confusion, when the King of Glory, in his powerful Word and Spirit, came to create new worlds:

> *On heavenly ground they stood; and from the shore*
> *They view'd the vast immeasurable abyss*
> *Outrageous as a sea, dark, wasteful, wild,*
> *Up from the bottom turn'd by furious winds*
> *And surging waves, as mountains, to assault*
> *Heaven's height, and with the center mix the pole.*
>
> *"Silence ye troubled waves, and thou deep, peace,"*
> *Said then the Omnific Word; "Your discord end."*
> *Then on the watery calm*
> *His brooding wings the Spirit of God outspread*
> *And vital virtue infused, and vital warmth*
> *Throughout the fluid mass.*

This, you see then, is the power of the Spirit. Could we have seen that earth, all in confusion, we should have said, "Who can make a world out of this?" The answer would have been,

> The power of the Spirit can do it. By the simple spreading of his dove-like wings he can make all the things come together. Upon that there shall be order where there was nought but confusion.

Nor is this all the power of the Spirit. We have seen some of his works in creation.

But there was one particular instance of creation in which the Holy Spirit was more especially concerned, viz., the formation of the body of our Lord Jesus Christ. Though our Lord Jesus Christ was born of a woman and made in the likeness of sinful flesh, yet the power that begat him was entirely in God the Holy Spirit—as the Scriptures express it, "The power of the Highest shall overshadow thee." He was *begotten,* as the Apostles' Creed says, begotten of the Holy Ghost. "That holy thing which is born of thee shall be called the Son of the Highest." The corporeal frame of the Lord Jesus Christ was a masterpiece of the Holy Spirit. I suppose his body to have excelled all others in beauty; to have been like that of the first man, the very pattern of what the body is to be in Heaven, when it shall shine forth in all its glory. That fabric, in all its beauty and perfection, was modeled by the Spirit. In his book were all the members written when as yet there were none of them. He fashioned and formed him; and here again we have another instance of the creative energy of the Spirit.

2. A second manifestation of the Holy Spirit's power is to be found in the *resurrection of the Lord Jesus Christ.* If ye have ever studied this subject, ye have perhaps been rather perplexed to find that sometimes the resurrection of Christ is ascribed to himself. By his own power and Godhead he could not be held by the bond of death, but as he willingly gave up his life, he had power to take it again. In another portion of Scripture you find it ascribed to God the Father: "He raised him up from the dead;" "Him hath God the Father exalted." And many other passages of similar import. But, again, it is said in Scripture that Jesus Christ was raised by the Holy Spirit. Now all these things were true. He was raised by the Father because the Father said, "Loose the prisoner—let him go. Justice is satisfied. My law requires no more satisfaction—vengeance has had its due—let him go." Here he gave an official message which delivered Jesus from the grave. He was raised by his own majesty and power because he had a right to come out, and he felt he had, and therefore "burst the bonds of death: he could be no longer holden of them." But, he was raised by the Spirit as to that energy which his mortal frame received, by the which it rose again from the grave after having lain there for three days and nights. If you want proofs of this, you must open your Bibles again—1 Peter 3:18.

> For Christ also hath once suffered for sins, the just for the unjust, that he might bring us to God, being put to death in the flesh but quickened by the Spirit.

And a further proof you may find in Romans 8:11. (I love sometimes to be textual, for I believe the great fault of Christians is that they do not search the Scriptures enough, and I will make them search them when they are here if they do not do so anywhere else.)

> But if the Spirit of him that raised up Jesus from the dead dwell in you, he that raised up Christ from the dead shall also quicken your mortal bodies by his Spirit that dwelleth in you.

The resurrection of Christ, then, was effected by the agency of the Spirit, and here we have a noble illustration of his omnipotence. Could you have stepped, as angels did, into the grave of Jesus, and seen his sleeping body, you would have found it cold as any other corpse. Lift up the hand, it falls by the side. Look at the eye: it is glazed. And there is a death-thrust which must have annihilated life. See his hands; the blood distils not from them, they are cold and motionless. Can that body live? Can it start up? Yes; and be an illustration of the might of the Spirit. For when the power of the Spirit came on him, as it was when it fell upon the dry bones of the valley:

> He arose in the majesty of his divinity, and bright and shining, astonished the watchmen so that they fled away, yea, he arose no more to die, but to live forever, King of kings and Prince of the kings of the earth.

3. The third of the works of the Holy Spirit which have so wonderfully demonstrated his power, are *attestation works*. I mean by this, works of witnessing. When Jesus Christ went into the stream of baptism in the river Jordan, the Holy Spirit descended upon him like a dove, and proclaimed him God's beloved son. That was what I style an attestation work. And when afterwards Jesus Christ raised the dead, when he healed the leper, when he spoke to diseases and they fled apace, when demons rushed in thousands from those who were possessed of them, it was done by the power of the Spirit. The Spirit dwelt in Jesus without measure, and by that power all those miracles were worked. These were attestation works. And when Jesus Christ was gone, you will remember that master attestation of the Spirit when he came like a rushing mighty wind upon the assembled apostles, and cloven tongues sat upon them; and you will remember how he attested their ministry by giving them to speak with tongues as he gave them utterance; and how, also, miraculous deeds were wrought by them, how they taught, how Peter raised Dorcas how he breathed life into Eutycus, how great deeds were wrought by the apostles as well as their Master—so that "mighty signs and wonders were done by the Holy Ghost, and many believed thereby." Who will doubt the power of the Holy Spirit after that? Ah! those Socinians who deny the existence of the Holy Ghost and his absolute personality, what will

they do when we get them on creation, resurrection, and attestation? They must rush in the very teeth of Scripture. But mark! it is a stone upon which if any man fall he shall be bruised; but if it fall upon him, as it will do if he resists it, it shall grind him to powder. The Holy Spirit has power omnipotent, even the power of God.

4. Once more, if we want another outward and visible sign of the power of the Spirit, we may look at the *works of grace*. Behold a city where a soothsayer hath the power—who has given out himself to be some great one: a Philip enters it and preaches the Word of God—straightway a Simon Magus loses his power and himself seeks for the power of the Spirit to be given to him, fancying it might be purchased with money. See, in modern times, a country where the inhabitants live in miserable wigwams, feeding on reptiles and the meanest creatures; observe them bowing down before their idols and worshipping their false gods, and so plunged in superstition, so degraded and debased, that it became a question whether they had souls or not; behold a Moffat go with the Word of God in his hand, hear him preach as the Spirit gives him utterance, and accompanies that Word with power. They cast aside their idols—they hate and abhor their former lusts; they build houses, wherein they dwell; they become clothed, and in their right mind. They break the bow, and cut the spear in sunder; the uncivilized become civilized; the savage becomes polite; he who knew nothing begins to read the Scriptures, thus out of the mouths of Hottentots,[1] God attests the power of his mighty Spirit.

Take a household in this city—and we could guide you to many such—the father is a drunkard; he has been the most desperate of characters; see him in his madness, and you might just as well meet an unchained tiger as meet such a man. He seems as if he could rend a man to pieces who should offend him. Mark his wife. She, too, has a spirit in her, and when he treats her ill she can resist him; many broils have been seen in that house, and often has the neighborhood been disturbed by the noise created there. As for the poor little children—see them in their rags and nakedness, poor untaught things. Untaught, did I say? They are taught and well taught in the devil's school, and are growing up to be the heirs of damnation.

But someone whom God has blessed by his Spirit is guided to the house. He may be but a humble city missionary perhaps, but he speaks to such a one: "O," says he, "come and listen to the voice of God." Whether it is by his own agency, or a minister's preaching, the Word, which is quick and powerful, cuts to the sinner's heart. The tears run down his cheeks—such as had never been seen before. He shakes and quivers. The strong man bows down—the

---

[1] Hottentots: black Africans. (Derogative.)

mighty man trembles—and those knees that never shook, begin to knock together. That heart which never quailed before, now begins to shake before the power of the Spirit. He sits down on a humble bench by the penitent; he lets his knees bend, whilst his lips utter a child's prayer, but, whilst a child's prayer, a prayer of a child of God. He becomes a changed character. Mark the reformation in his house! That wife of his becomes the decent matron. Those children are the credit of the house, and in due time they grow up like olive branches round his table, adorning his house like polished stones. Pass by the house—no noise or broils, but songs of Zion. See him—no drunken revelry; he has drained his last cup; and, now forswearing it, he comes to God and is his servant. Now, you will not hear at midnight the bacchanalian shout; but should there be a noise, it will be the sound of the solemn hymn of praise to God. And, now, is there not, such a thing as the power of the Spirit? Yes! and these must have witnessed it and seen it. I know a village, [that was] once, perhaps, the most profane in England—a village inundated by drunkenness and debauchery of the worst kind, where it was impossible almost for an honest traveler to stop in the public house without being annoyed by blasphemy; a place noted for incendiaries and robbers. One man, the ringleader of all, listened to the voice of God. That man's heart was broken. The whole gang came to hear the gospel preached, and they sat and seemed to reverence the preacher as if he were a God, and not a man. These men became changed and reformed; and everyone who knows the place affirms that such a change had never been wrought but by the power of the Holy Ghost.

Let the gospel be preached and the Spirit poured out, and you will see that it has such power to change the conscience, to ameliorate the conduct, to raise the debased, to chastise and to curb the wickedness of the race, that you must glory in it. I say, there is naught like the power of the Spirit. Only let that come, and, indeed, everything can be accomplished.

II. Now, for the second point, *the inward and spiritual power of the Holy Spirit.*

What I have already spoken of may be seen; what I am about to speak of must be *felt*, and no man will apprehend what I say with truth unless he has felt it. The other, even the infidel must confess; the other, the greatest blasphemer cannot deny if he speaks the truth; but this is what the one will laugh at as enthusiasm and what the other will say is but the invention of our fevered fancies. However, we have a more sure word of testimony than all that they may say. We have a witness within. We know it is the truth, and we are not afraid to speak of the inward spiritual power of the Holy Ghost. Let us notice two or three things wherein the inward and spiritual power of the Holy Ghost is very greatly to be seen and extolled.

1. First, in that the Holy Ghost has *a power over men's hearts*. Now, men's hearts are very hard to affect. If you want to get at them for any worldly object, you can do it. A cheating world can win man's heart, a little gold can win man's heart, a trump of fame and a little clamor of applause can win man's heart. But there is not a minister breathing that can win man's heart himself. He can win his ears and make them listen; he can win his eyes, and fix those eyes upon him; he can win the attention—but the heart is very slippery. Yes, the heart is a fish that troubles all gospel fishermen to hold. You may sometimes pull it almost all out of the water; but slimy as an eel, it slippeth between your fingers, and you have not captured it after all. Many a man has fancied that he has caught the heart, but has been disappointed. It would need a strong hunter to overtake the hart on the mountains. It is too fleet for human foot to approach. The Spirit alone has power over man's heart.

Do you ever try your power on a heart? If any man thinks that a minister can convert the soul, I wish he would try. Let him go and be a Sabbath-school teacher. He shall take his class, he shall have the best books that can be obtained, he shall have the best rules, he shall draw his lines of circumvallation [defense] about his spiritual Sebastopol [besieged city], he shall take the best boy in his class—and if he is not tired in a week, I shall be very much mistaken. Let him spend four or five Sabbaths in trying, but he will say, "The young fellow is incorrigible." Let him try another. And he will have to try another, and another, and another, before he will manage to convert one. He will soon find "It is not by might nor by power, but by my Spirit," saith the Lord. Can a minister convert? Can he touch the heart? David said, "Your hearts are as fat as grease." Ay, that is quite true; and we cannot get through so much grease at all. Our sword cannot get at the heart, it is encased in so much fatness, it is harder than a nether millstone. Many a good old Jerusalem blade has been blunted against the hard heart. Man, a piece of the true steel that God has put into the hands of his servants, has had the edge turned by being set up against the sinner's heart. We cannot reach the soul; but the Holy Spirit can. "My beloved can put in his hand by the hole in the door and my bowels will move for sin." He can give a sense of blood-bought pardon that shall dissolve a heart of stone. He can . . .

> *Speak with that voice which wakes the dead,*
> *And bids the sinner rise:*
> *And makes the guilty conscience dread*
> *The death that never dies.*

He can make Sinai's thunders audible; yea, and he can make the sweet whisperings of Calvary enter into the soul. He has power over the heart of man. And here is a glorious proof of the omnipotence of the Spirit that he has rule over the heart.

2. But if there is one thing more stubborn than the heart, it is *the will*. "My lord; Will-be-will," as Bunyan calls him in his *Holy War*, is a fellow who will not easily be bent. The will, especially in some men, is a very stubborn thing, and in all men, if the will is once stirred up to opposition, there is nothing can be done with them.

Freewill, somebody believes in. *Freewill,* many dream of. Freewill! Wherever is that to be found? Once there was free will in Paradise, and a terrible mess free will made there, for it all spoiled all Paradise and turned Adam out of the garden. Free will was once in Heaven, but it turned the glorious archangel out and a third part of the stars of Heaven fell into the abyss. I want nothing to do with free will, but I will try to see whether I have got a free will within. And I find I have. Very free will to evil, but very poor will to that which is good. Free will enough when I sin, but when I would do good, evil is present with me, and how to do that which I would, I find not. Yet some boast of free will. I wonder whether those who believe in it have any more power over persons wills than I have. I know I have not any. I find the old proverb very true, "One man can bring a horse to the water, but a hundred cannot make him drink." I find that I can bring you all to the water, and a great many more than can get into this chapel; but I cannot make you drink; and I don't think a hundred ministers could make you drink. I have read old Rowland Hill, and Whitfield, and several others to see what they did; but I cannot discover a plan of turning your wills. I cannot coax you; and you will not yield by any manner of means. I do not think any man has power over his fellow-creature's will, but the Spirit of God has. "I will make them willing in the day of my power." He maketh the unwilling sinner so willing that he is impetuous after the gospel; he who was obstinate, now hurries to the cross. He who laughed at Jesus, now hangs on his mercy; and he who would not believe, is now made by the Holy Spirit to do it, not only willingly, but eagerly; he is happy, is glad to do it, rejoices in the sound of Jesus' name, and delights to run in the way of God's commandments. The Holy Spirit has power over the will.

3. And yet there is one thing more which I think is *rather worse than the will*. You will guess what I mean. The will is somewhat worse than the heart to bend, but there is one thing that excels the will in its naughtiness, and that is the *imagination*. I hope that my will is managed by Divine Grace. But I am afraid my imagination is not at times. Those who have a fair share of imagination know what a difficult thing it is to control. You cannot restrain it. It will break the reins. You will never be able to manage it. The imagination will sometimes fly up to God with such a power that eagles' wings cannot match it. It sometimes has such might that it can almost see the King in his beauty, and the land which is very far off. With regard to myself, my imagination will sometimes take me over the gates of iron, across that infinite unknown, to the very gates of pearl, and discovers the blessed glorified.

But if it is potent one way, it is [also in] another; for my imagination has taken me down to the vilest kennels and sewers of earth. It has given me thoughts so dreadful that, while I could not avoid them, yet I was thoroughly horrified at them. These thoughts will come, and when I feel in the holiest frame, the most devoted to God, and the most earnest in prayer, it often happens that that is the very time when the plagues breaks out the worst. But I rejoice and think of one thing, that I can cry out when this imagination comes upon me. I know it is said in the book of Leviticus, when an act of evil was committed, if the maiden cried out against it, then her life was to be spared. So it is with the Christian. If he cries out there is hope. Can you chain your imagination? No; but the power of the Holy Ghost can. Ah, it shall do it, and it does do it at last; it does it, even on earth.

III. But the last thing was *the future and desired effects*—for, after all, though the Holy Spirit has done so much, he cannot say, "It is finished."

Jesus Christ could exclaim concerning his own labor—"It is finished." But the Holy Spirit cannot say that. He has more to do yet: and until the consummation of all things, when the Son himself becomes subject to the Father, it shall not be said by the Holy Spirit, "It is finished." What, then, has the Holy Spirit to do?

1. First, he has to *perfect us in holiness*. There are two kinds of perfection which a Christian needs—one is the perfection of justification in the person of Jesus; and the other is, the perfection of sanctification worked in him by the Holy Spirit. At present, corruption still rests even in the breasts of the regenerate. At present the heart is partially impure. At present there are still lusts and evil imaginations. But, Oh! my soul rejoices to know that the day is coming when God shall finish the work which he has begun; and he shall present my soul, not only perfect in Christ, but, perfect in the Spirit, without spot or blemish, or any such thing. And is it true that this poor depraved heart is to become as holy as that of God? And is it true that this poor spirit, which often cries, "O wretched man that I am, who shall deliver me from the body of this sin and death!" shall get rid of sin and death—I shall have no evil things to vex my ears, and no unholy thoughts to disturb my peace? Oh! happy hour! may it be hastened! Just before I die, sanctification will be finished; but not till that moment shall I ever claim perfection in myself. But at that moment when I depart, my spirit shall have its last baptism in the Holy Spirit's fire. It shall be put in the crucible for its last trying in the furnace; and then, free from all dross, and fine like a wedge of pure gold, it shall be presented at the feet of God without the least degree of dross or mixture. O glorious hour! O blessed moment! Methinks I long to die [even] if there were no Heaven, if I might but have that last purification, and come up from Jordan's stream most white from the washing. Oh! to be washed white, clean, pure, perfect! Not an angel more pure than I shall be—yea, not God himself more holy! And I shall be able to say, in a double sense, "Great God, I am clean—through Jesus's blood I am clean, through the Spirit's work, I am clean too!" Must we not extol the power of the Holy Ghost in thus making us fit to stand before our Father in Heaven?

2. Another great work of the Holy Spirit which is not accomplished is *the bringing on of the latter-day glory*. In a few more years—I know not when, I know not how—the Holy Spirit will be poured out in a far different style from the present. There are diversities of operations; and during the last few years it has been the case that the diversified operations have consisted in very little pouring out of the Spirit. Ministers have gone on in dull routine, continually preaching, preaching, preaching—and little good has been done. I do hope that perhaps a fresh era has dawned upon us, and that there is a better pouring out of the Spirit even now. For the hour is coming, and it may be even now is, when the Holy Ghost shall be poured out again in such a wonderful manner that many shall run to and fro, and knowledge shall be increased—the knowledge of the Lord shall cover the earth as the waters cover the surface of the great deep, when his kingdom shall come, and his will shall be done on earth even as it is in Heaven. We are not going to be dragging on forever like Pharoah, with the wheels off his chariot. My heart exults and my eyes flash with the thought that very likely I shall live to see the out-pouring of the Spirit when "the sons and the daughters of God again shall prophecy, and the young men shall see visions, and the old men shall dream dreams." Perhaps there shall be no miraculous gifts, for they will not be required; but yet there shall be such a miraculous amount of holiness, such an extraordinary fervor of prayer, such a real communion with God and so much vital religion, and such a spread of the doctrines of the cross, that everyone will see that verily the Spirit is poured out like water and the rains are descending from above. For that let us pray: let us continually labor for it, and seek it of God.

3. One more work of the Spirit which will especially manifest his power—*the general resurrection*. We have reason to believe from Scripture that the resurrection of the dead, whilst it will be effected by the voice of God and of his Word (the Son), shall also be brought about by the Spirit. That same power which raised Jesus Christ from the dead, shall also quicken your mortal bodies. The power of the resurrection is perhaps one of the finest proofs of the works of the Spirit. Ah! my friends, if this earth could but have its mantle torn away for a little while, if the green sod could be cut from it, and we could look about six feet deep into its bowels, what a world it would seem! What should we see? Bones, carcasses, rottenness, worms, corruption. And you would say, "Can these dry bones live? Can they start up?" "Yes! in a moment! in the twinkling of an eye, at the last trump, the dead shall be raised." He speaks: they are alive! See them scattered: bone comes to his bone! See them naked: flesh comes upon them! See them still lifeless: "Come from the four winds, O breath, and breathe upon these slain!" When the wind of the Holy Spirit comes, they live, and they stand upon their feet an exceeding great army.

I have thus attempted to speak of the power of the Spirit, and I trust I have shown it to you. We must now have a moment or two for practical inference. The

Spirit is very powerful, Christian! What do you infer from that fact? Why, that you never need distrust the power of God to carry you to Heaven. O how that sweet verse was laid to my soul yesterday:

> His tried Almighty arm
> Is raised for your defense;
> Where is the power [that] can reach you there?
> Or what can pluck you thence?

The power of the Holy Spirit is your bulwark, and all his omnipotence defends you. Can your enemies overcome omnipotence? Then they can conquer you. Can they wrestle with Diety, and hurl him to the ground? Then they might conquer you. For the power of the Spirit is *our* power; the power of the Spirit is *our* might.

Once again, Christians, if this is the power of the Spirit, *why should you doubt anything?* There is your son. There is that wife of yours, for whom you have supplicated so frequently: do not doubt the Spirit's power. "Though he tarry, wait for him." There is thy husband, O holy woman! and thou hast wrestled for his soul. And though he is ever so hardened and desperate a wretch, and treats thee ill, there is power in the Spirit. And, O ye who have come from barren churches with scarcely a leaf upon the tree: do not doubt the power of the Spirit to raise you up. For it shall be a "pasture for flocks, a den of wild asses," open, but deserted, until the Spirit is poured out from on high. And then the parched ground shall be made a pool, and the thirsty land springs of water, and in the habitations of dragons, where each lay shall be grass with reeds and rushes. And, O ye members of Park Street [Chapel], ye who remember what your God has done for you: especially never distrust the power of the Spirit. Ye have seen the wilderness blossom like Carmel, ye have seen the desert blossom like the rose; trust him for the future. Then go out and labor with this conviction, that the power of the Holy Ghost is able to do anything. Go to your Sunday-school; go to your tract distribution; go to your missionary enterprise, go to your preaching in your rooms, with the conviction that the power of the Spirit is our great help.

And now, lastly, to you sinners: what is there to be said to you about this power of the Spirit? Why, to me, there is some hope for some of you. I cannot save you: I cannot get at you. I make you cry sometimes—you wipe your eyes, and it is all over. But I know my Master can. That is my consolation. Chief of sinners, there is hope for thee! This power can save you as well as anybody else. It is able to break your heart, though it is an iron one; to make your eyes run with tears though they have been like rocks before. His power is able this morning, if he will, to change your heart, to turn the current of all your ideas, to make you at once a child of God, to justify you in Christ. There is power enough in the Holy Spirit. Ye are not straitened [in distress] in *Him,* but in your own bowels [strength]. He is able to bring sinners to Jesus: he is able to make you willing in the day of his power. Are you willing this morning? Has he gone so far as to make you desire his name, to make you wish for Jesus? Then, O sinner! whilst he draws you, say, "Draw me, I am wretched without thee." Follow him, follow him, and, while he leads, tread you in his footsteps, and rejoice that he has begun a good work in you, for there is an evidence that he will continue it even unto the end. And, O desponding one! put thy trust in the power of the Spirit. Rest on the blood of Jesus, and thy soul is safe, not only now, but throughout eternity. God bless you, my hearers. Amen.

The Holy Ghost, the Great Teacher

Delivered on Sabbath morning, November 18, 1855, at New Park Street Chapel, Southwark. No. 50.

Howbeit when he, the Spirit of truth, is come, he will guide you into all truth: for he shall not speak of himself; but whatsoever he shall hear, that shall he speak: and he will shew you things to come.—John 16:13

This generation hath gradually, and almost imperceptibly, become to a great extent a godless generation. One of the diseases of the present generation of mankind is their secret but deep-seated godlessness, by which they have so far departed from the knowledge of God. Science has discovered to us second causes; and hence, many have too much forgotten the first Great Cause, the Author of all: they have been able so far to pry into secrets, that the great axiom of the existence of a God has been too much neglected. Even among professing Christians, while there is a great amount of religion, there is too little godliness: there is much external formalism, but too little inward acknowledgment of God, too little living on God, living with God, and relying upon God. Hence arises the sad fact that when you enter many of our places of worship you will certainly hear the name of God mentioned; but except in the benediction, you would scarcely know there was a Trinity. In many places dedicated to Jehovah, the name of Jesus is too often kept in the background; the Holy Spirit is almost entirely neglected; and very little is said concerning his sacred influence. Even religious men have become to a large degree godless in this age. We sadly require more preaching regarding God; more preaching of those things which look not so much at the creature to be saved, as at God the Great One, to be extolled. My firm conviction is that, in proportion as we have more regard for the sacred godhead, the wondrous Trinity in Unity—shall we see a greater display of God's power, and a more glorious manifestation of his might in our churches. May God send us Christ-exalting, Spirit-loving ministry-men who shall proclaim God the Holy Ghost in all his offices, and shall extol God the Savior as the author and finisher of our faith, not neglecting that Great God, the Father of his people, who, before all worlds, elected us in Christ his Son, justified us through his righteousness, and will inevitably preserve us and gather us together in one, in the consummation of all things at the last great day.

Our text has regard to God the Holy Spirit; of him we shall speak and him only, if his sweet influence shall rest upon us.

The disciples had been instructed by Christ concerning certain elementary doctrines, but Jesus did not teach his disciples more than what we should call the "A-B-Cs" of religion. He gives his reasons for this in the 12th verse: "I have yet many things to say unto you, but you cannot bear them now." His disciples were not possessors of the Spirit. They had the Spirit so far as the work of conversion was concerned, but not as to the matters of bright illumination, profound instruction, prophecy, and inspiration. He says,

> I am now about to depart, and when I go from you I will send the Comforter unto you. Ye cannot bear these things now: howbeit, when he, the Spirit of truth is come, he will guide you into all truth.

The same promise that he made to his apostles, stands good to all his children; and in reviewing it, we shall take it as our portion and heritage, and shall not consider ourselves intruders upon the manor of the apostles, or upon their exclusive rights and prerogatives; for we conceive that Jesus says even to us, "When he, the Spirit of truth is come, he will guide you into all truth."

Dwelling exclusively upon our text, we have five things. First of all, here is *an attainment mentioned*—a knowledge of all truth; secondly, here is *a difficulty suggested*—which is, that we need guidance into all truth; thirdly, here is *a person provided*—"when he, the Spirit shall come, he shall guide you into all truth;" fourthly, here is *a manner hinted at*—"he shall guide you into all truth;" fifthly, here is *a sign given as to the working of the Spirit*—we may know whether he works, by his "guiding us into *all* truth"—into all of *one thing*; not *truths*, but *truth*.

I. Here is *an attainment mentioned,* which is a knowledge of all truth.

We know that some conceive doctrinal knowledge to be of very little importance, and of no practical use. We do not think so. We believe the science of Christ crucified and a judgment of the teachings of Scripture to be exceedingly valuable; we think it is right, that the Christian ministry should not only be arousing but instructing; not merely awakening, but enlightening: that it should appeal not only to the passions but to the understanding. We are far from thinking doctrinal knowledge to be of secondary importance; we believe it to be one of the first things in the Christian life, to know the truth, and then to practice it. We scarcely need this morning tell you how desirable it is for us to be well taught in things of the kingdom.

First of all, *nature itself,* (when it has been sanctified by grace,) *gives us a strong desire to know all truth.* The natural man separateth himself and intermeddleth with all knowledge. God has put an instinct in him by which he is rendered unsatisfied if he cannot probe mystery to its bottom; he can never be content until he can unriddle secrets. What we call curiosity is something given us of God impelling us to search into the knowledge of natural things; that curiosity, sanctified by the Spirit, is also brought to bear in matters of heavenly science and celestial wisdom. "Bless the Lord," said David, "O my soul, and *all that is within me* bless his holy name!" If there is a curiosity within us, it ought to be employed and developed in a search after truth. "All that is within me," sanctified by the Spirit, should be developed, And, verily, the Christian man feels an intense longing to bury his ignorance and receive wisdom. If he, when in his natural estate, panted for terrestrial knowledge, how much more ardent is the wish to unravel, if possible, the sacred mysteries of God's Word! A true Christian is always intently reading and searching the Scripture that he may be able to certify himself as to its main and cardinal truths. I do not think much of that man who does not wish to understand doctrines; I cannot conceive him to be in a right position when he thinks it is no matter whether he believes a lie or truth, whether he is heretic or orthodox, whether he received the Word of God as it is written, or as it is diluted and misconstrued by man. God's Word will ever be to a Christian a source of great anxiety; a sacred instinct within will lead him to pry into it; he will seek to understand it. Oh! there are some who forget this, men who purposely abstain from mentioning what are called high doctrines, because they think if they should mention high doctrines they would be dangerous; so they keep them back. Foolish men! They do not know anything of human nature; for if they did understand a grain's worth of humanity, they would know that the hiding of these things impels men to search them out. From the fact that they do not mention them, they drive men to places where these, and these only, are preached. They say, "If I preach election, and predestination, and these dark things, people will all go straight away, and become Antinomians."[1] I am not so sure if they were to be called Antinomians it would hurt them much; but hear me, oh, ye ministers that conceal these truths: that is the way to make them Antinomians, by silencing these doctrines. Curiosity is strong; if you tell them they

---

[1] Antinomians: A group opposed to or denying the fixed meaning or universal applicability of moral law. (*American Heritage Dictionary,* 4th Edition, 2000.)

must not pluck the truth, they will be sure to do it; but if you give it to them as you find it in God's Word, they will not seek to "wrest" it. Enlightened men *will* have the truth, and if they see election in Scripture, they will say, *"it is there,* and I will find it out. If I cannot get it in one place, I will get it in another." The true Christian has an inward longing and anxiety after it; he is hungry and thirsty after the word of righteousness, and he must and will feed on this bread of heaven, or at all hazards he will leave the husks which unsound divines would offer him.

Not only is this attainment to be desired because nature teaches us so, but a knowledge of all truth is *very essential for our comfort.* I do believe that many persons have been distressed half their lives from the fact that they had not clear views of truth. Many poor souls, for instance, under conviction, abide three or four times as long in sorrow of mind as they would require [need] to do if they had someone to instruct them in the great matter of justification. So there are believers who are often troubling themselves about falling away; but if they knew in their soul the great consolation that we are kept by the grace of God through faith unto salvation, they would be no more troubled about it. So have I found some distressed about the unpardonable sin—but if God instructs us in that doctrine, and shows us that no conscience that is really awakened ever can commit that sin, but that when it is committed, God gives us up to a seared conscience, so that we never fear or tremble afterwards—all that distress would be alleviated. Depend on this, the more you know of God's truth—all things else being equal—the more comfortable you will be as a Christian. Nothing can give a greater light on your path than a clear understanding of divine things. It is a mingle-mangled gospel too commonly preached, which causes the downcast faces of Christians. Give me the congregation whose faces are bright with joy, let their eyes glisten at the sound of the gospel, then will I believe that it is God's own words they are receiving. Instead thereof you will often see melancholy congregations whose visages are not much different from the bitter countenance of poor creatures swallowing medicine, because the word spoken terrifies them by its legality, instead of comforting them by its grace. We love a cheerful gospel, and we think "all the truth" will tend to comfort the Christian.

"Comfort again," says another, "always comfort." Ah, but there is another reason why we prize truth, because we believe that a true knowledge of all the truth *will keep us very much out of danger.* No doctrine is so calculated to preserve a man from sin as the doctrine of the grace of God. Those who have called it a licentious doctrine did not know anything at all about it. Poor ignorant things, they little knew that their own vile stuff was the most licentious doctrine under Heaven. If they knew the grace of God in truth, they would soon see that there was no preservative from lying like a knowledge that we are elect of God from the foundation of the world. There is nothing like a belief in my eternal perseverance, and the immutability of my Father's affection, which can keep me near to him from a motive of simple gratitude. Nothing makes a man so virtuous as belief of truth. A lying doctrine will soon beget a lying practice. A man cannot have an erroneous belief without by-and-bye having an erroneous life. I believe the one thing naturally begets the other. Keep near God's truth; keep near his word; keep the head right, and especially keep your heart right with regard to truth, and your feet will not go far astray.

Again, I hold also that this attainment to the knowledge of all truth is very desirable for *the usefulness which it will give us in the world at large*. We should not be selfish: we should always consider whether a thing will be beneficial to others. A knowledge of all truth will make us very serviceable in this world. We shall be skillful physicians who know how to take the poor distressed soul aside, to put the finger on his eye, and take the scale off for him, that heaven's light may comfort him. There will be no character, however perplexing may be its peculiar phase, but we shall be able to speak to it and comfort it. He who holds the truth, is usually the most useful man. As a good Presbyterian brother said to me the other day:

> I know God has blessed you exceedingly in gathering in souls, but it is an extraordinary fact that nearly all the men I know—with scarcely an exception—who have been made useful in gathering in souls, have held the great doctrines of the grace of God.

Almost every man whom God has blessed to the building up of the church in prosperity, and around whom the people have rallied, has been a man who has held firmly free grace from first to last, through the finished salvation of Christ. Do not you think you need have errors in your doctrine to make you useful. We have some who preach Calvinism all the first part of the sermon, and finish up with Arminianism, because they think that will make them useful. Useful nonsense! That is all it is. A man, if he cannot be useful with the truth, cannot be useful with an error. There is enough in the pure doctrine of God, without introducing heresies to preach to sinners. As far as I know, I never felt hampered or cramped in addressing the ungodly in my life. I can speak with as much fervency, and yet not in the same style as those who hold the contrary views of God's truth. Those who hold God's word, never need add something untrue in speaking to men. The sturdy truth of God touches every chord in every man's heart. If we can, by God's grace, put our hand inside man's heart, we want nothing but that whole truth to move him thoroughly, and to stir him up. There is nothing like the real truth and the whole truth, to make a man useful.

II. Now, again, here is a *difficulty suggested,* and that is—that we require a guide to conduct us into all truth.

The difficulty is that truth is not so easy to discover. There is no man born in this world by nature who has the truth in his heart. There is no creature that ever was fashioned, since the fall, who has a knowledge of truth innate and natural. It has been disputed by many philosophers whether there are such things as innate ideas at all; but [it] is of no use disputing as to whether there are any innate ideas of truth. There are none such. There are ideas of everything that is wrong and evil; but in us—that is, our flesh—there dwelleth no *good* thing: we are born in sin, and shapened in iniquity; in sin did our mother conceive us. There is nothing in us good, and no tendency to righteousness. Then, since we are not born with the truth, we have the task of searching for it. If we are to be blest by being eminently useful as Christian men, we must be well instructed in matters of revelation; but here is the difficulty—that we cannot follow without a guide the winding paths of truth. Why [is] this?

First, because of *the very great intricacy of truth itself.* Truth itself is no easy thing to discover. Those who fancy they know everything and constantly dogmatise with the spirit of "We are the men, and wisdom will die with us," of course see no difficulties whatever in the system they hold; but I believe, the most earnest student of Scripture will find things in the Bible which puzzle him; however earnestly he reads it, he will see some mysteries too deep for him to understand. He will cry out "Truth! I cannot find thee; I know not where thou art, thou art beyond me; I cannot fully view thee." Truth is a path so narrow that two can scarce walk together in it; we usually tread the narrow way in single file—two men can seldom walk arm in arm in the truth. We believe the same truth in the main, but we cannot walk together in the path, it is too narrow. The way of truth is very difficult. If you step an inch aside on the right you are in a dangerous error, and if you swerve a little to the left you are equally in the mire. On the one hand there is a huge precipice, and on the other a deep morass; and unless you keep to the true line, to the breadth of a hair, you will go astray. Truth is a narrow path indeed. It is a path the eagle's eye hath not seen, and a depth the diver hath not visited. It is like the veins of metal in a mine, it is often of excessive thinness, and moreover it runneth not in one continued layer. Lose it once, and you may dig for miles and not discover it again; the eye must watch perpetually the direction of the lode. Grains of truth are like the grains of gold in the rivers of Australia—they must be shaken by the hand of patience, and washed in the stream of honesty, or the fine gold will be mingled with sand. Truth is often mingled with error, and it is hard to distinguish it; but we bless God [that] it is said, "When the Spirit of truth is come, he will guide you into all truth."

Another reason why we need a guide is *the invidiousness of error*. It busily steals upon us, and, if I may so describe our position, we are often like we were on Thursday night in that tremendous fog. Most of us were feeling for ourselves, and wondering where on earth we were. We could scarcely see an inch before us. We came to a place where there were three turnings. We thought we knew the old spot. There was the lamp-post, and now we must take a sharp turn to the left; but not so. We ought to have gone a little to the right. We have been so often to the same place that we think we know every flag-stone—and there's our friend's shop over the way. It is dark, but we think we must be quite right, and all the while we are quite wrong, and find ourselves half-a-mile out of the way. So it is with matters of truth. We think, surely this is the right path; and the voice of the evil one whispers, "that is the way, walk ye in it." You do so, and you find to your great dismay, that instead of the path of truth, you have been walking in the paths of unrighteousness and erroneous doctrines. The way of life is a labyrinth; the grassiest paths and the most bewitching, are the farthest away from right; the most enticing, are those which are garnished with wrested truths. I believe there is not a counterfeit coin in the world so much like a genuine one as some errors are like the truth. One is base metal, the other is true gold; still, in externals they differ very little.

We also need a guide, because *we are so prone to go astray*. Why, if the path of Heaven were as straight as Bunyan pictures it, with no turning to the right hand or left—and no doubt it is—we are [still] so prone to go astray, that we should go to the right hand to the Mountains of Destruction, or to the left in the dark Wood of Desolation. David says, "I have gone astray like a lost sheep." That means very often: for if a sheep is put into a field twenty times, if it does not get out twenty-one times, it will be because it cannot; because the place is hurdled up, and it cannot find a hole in the hedge. If grace did not guide a man, he would go astray, though there were hand-posts all the way to Heaven. Let it be written, "*Miklat, Miklat,* the way to refuge." [Still] he would turn aside, and the avenger of blood would overtake him, if some guide did not, like the angels in Sodom, put his hand on his shoulders, and cry, "Escape, escape, for thy life! Look not behind thee; stay not in all the plain." These, then, are the reasons why we need a guide.

III. In the third place, here is *a person provided*.

This is none other than God, and this God is none other than a person. This person is "he, the Spirit," the "Spirit of truth"—not an influence or an emanation, but actually a person. "When the Spirit of truth is come, he shall guide you into all truth." Now, we wish you to look at this guide to consider how adapted he is to us.

In the first place, he is *infallible*; he knows everything and cannot lead us astray. If I pin my sleeve to another man's coat, he may lead me part of the way rightly, but by-and-bye he will go wrong himself, and I shall be led astray with him; but if I give myself to the Holy Ghost and ask his guidance, there is no fear of my wandering.

Again, we rejoice in this Spirit because he is *ever-present*. We fall into a difficulty sometimes; we say, "Oh, if I could take this to my minister, he would explain it; but I live so far off, and am not able to see him." That perplexes us, and we turn the text round and round and cannot make anything out of it. We look at the commentators. We take down pious Thomas Scott, and, as usual he says nothing about it if it be a dark passage. Then we go to holy Matthew Henry, and if it is an easy Scripture, he is sure to explain it; but if it is a text hard to be understood, it is likely enough, of course, left in his own gloom; and even Dr. Gill himself, the most consistent of commentators, when he comes to a hard passage, manifestly avoids it in some degree. But when we have no commentator or minister, we have still the Holy Spirit; and let me tell you a little secret: whenever you cannot understand a text, open your Bible, bend your knee, and pray over that text; and if it does not split into atoms and open itself, try again. If prayer does not explain it, it is one of the things God did not intend you to know, and you may be content to be ignorant of it. Prayer is the key that openeth the cabinets of mystery. Prayer and faith are sacred picklocks that can open secrets, and obtain great treasures. There is no college for holy education like that of the blessed Spirit, for he is an ever—present tutor, to whom we have only to bend the knee, and he is at our side, the great expositor of truth.

But there is one thing about the suitability of this guide which is remarkable. I do not know whether it has struck you—the Holy Spirit can "guide us *into* a truth." Now, man can guide us *to* a truth, but it is only the Holy Spirit who can "guide us *into* a truth." "When he, the Spirit of truth, shall come, he shall guide you *into*"—mark that word—"all truth." Now, for instance, it is a long while before you can lead some people to election; but when you have made them see its correctness, you have not led them "into" it. You may show them that it is plainly stated in Scripture, but they will turn away and hate it. You take them to another great truth, but they have been brought up in a different fashion, and though they cannot answer your arguments, they say, "The man is right, perhaps," and they whisper—but so low that conscience itself cannot hear—"but it is so contrary to my prejudices, that I cannot receive it." After you have led them *to* the truth, and they see it is true, how hard it is to lead them *into* it! There are many of my hearers who are brought *to* the truth of their depravity, but they are not brought *into* it, and made to feel it. Some of you are brought to know the truth that God keeps us from day to day; but you rarely get into it, so as to live in continual dependence upon God the Holy Ghost, and draw fresh supplies from him. The thing is, to get inside it. A Christian should do with truth as a snail does with his shell—live inside it, as well as carry it on his back, and bear it perpetually about with him. The Holy Ghost, it is said, shall lead us into all truth. You may be brought to a chamber where there is an abundance of gold and silver, but you will be no richer unless you effect an entrance. It is the Spirit's work to unbar the two leaved gates, and bring us into truth, so that we may get inside it, and, as dear old Rowland Hill said, "Not only hold the truth, but have the truth hold us."

IV. Fourthly, here is a *method suggested*: "He shall guide you into all truth."

Now I must have an illustration. I must compare truth to some cave or grotto that you have heard of, with wondrous stalactites hanging from the roof, and others starting from the floor; a cavern, glittering with spar and abounding in marvels. Before entering the cavern you inquire for a guide, who comes with his lighted flambeau. He conducts you down to a considerable depth, and you find yourself in the midst of the cave. He leads you through different chambers. Here he points to a little stream rushing from amid the rocks, and indicates its rise and progress; there he points to some peculiar rock and tells you its name; then takes you into a large natural hall, tells you how many persons once feasted in it; and so on. Truth is a grand series of caverns, it is our glory to have so great and wise a conductor. Imagine that we are coming to the darkness of it. He is a light shining in the midst of us to guide us; and by the light he shows us wondrous things. In three ways the Holy Ghost teaches us: by suggestion, direction, and illumination.

First, he guides us into all truth *by suggesting it*. There are thoughts that dwell in our minds that were not born there, but which were exotics brought from Heaven and put there by the Spirit. It is not a fancy that angels whisper into our ears, and that devils do the same: both good and evil spirits hold converse with men; and some of us have known it. We have had strange thoughts which were not the offspring of our souls, but which came from angelic visitants; and direct temptations and evil insinuations have we had which were not brewed in our own souls, but which came from the pestilential cauldron of Hell. So the Spirit doth speak in men's ears, sometimes in the darkness of the night. In ages gone by he spoke in dreams and visions, but now he speaketh by his Word. Have you not at times had unaccountably, in the middle of your business, a thought concerning God and heavenly things, and could not tell whence it came? Have you not been reading or studying the Scripture, but a text came across your mind, and you could not help it; though you even put it down, it was like cork in water, and would swim up again to the top of your mind. Well, that good thought was put there by the Spirit; he often guides his people into all truth by suggesting, just as the guide in the grotto does with his flambeau. He does not say a word, perhaps, but he walks into a passage himself, and you follow him: so the Spirit suggests a thought, and your heart follows it up. Well can I remember the manner in which I learned the doctrines of grace in a single instant. Born, as all of us are by nature, an Arminian, I still believed the old things I had heard continually from the pulpit, and did not see the grace of God. I remember sitting one day in the house of God and hearing a sermon as dry as possible, and as worthless as all such sermons are, when a thought struck my mind—"How came I to be converted?" "I prayed," thought I. Then I thought, "How came I to pray?" "I was induced to pray by reading the Scriptures." "How came I to read the Scriptures?" "Why—I did read them, and what led me to that?" And then, in a moment, I saw that God was at the bottom of all, and that he was the author of faith; and then the whole doctrine opened up to me, from which I have not departed.

But sometimes he leads us *by direction*. The guide points and says—"There, gentlemen, go along that particular path, that is the way." So the Spirit gives a direction and tendency to our thoughts; not suggesting a new one but letting a particular thought, when it starts, take such-and-such a direction; not so much putting a boat on the stream, as steering it when it is there. When our thoughts are considering sacred things, he leads us into a more excellent channel from that in which we started. Time after time have you commenced a meditation on a certain doctrine and, unaccountably, you were gradually led away into another, and you saw how one doctrine leaned on another, as is the case with the stones in the arch of a bridge, all hanging on the keystone of Jesus Christ crucified. You were brought to see these things, not by a new idea suggested, but by direction given to your thoughts.

But perhaps the best way in which the Holy Ghost leads us into all truth is by *illumination*. He illuminates the Bible. Now, have any of you an illuminated Bible at home? "No," says one, "I have a morocco Bible; I have a polyglot [multi-language] Bible; I have a marginal reference Bible." Ah! that is all very well, but have you an *illuminated* Bible? "Yes, I have a large family Bible with pictures in it." There is a picture of John the Baptist baptizing Christ by pouring water on his head, and many other nonsensical things; but that is not what I mean: have you an *illuminated* Bible? "Yes, I have a Bible with splendid engravings in it." Yes; I know you may have; but have you an *illuminated* Bible? "I don't understand what you mean by an illuminated Bible." Well, it is the Christian man who has an illuminated Bible. He does not buy it illuminated originally, but when he reads it . . .

> *A glory gilds the sacred page,*
> *Majestic like the sun*
> *Which gives a light to every age,*
> *—It gives, but borrows none.*

There is nothing like reading an illuminated Bible, beloved. You may read to all eternity, and never learn anything by it, unless it is illuminated by the Spirit; and then the words shine forth like stars. The book seems made of gold leaf; every single letter glitters like a diamond. Oh, it is a blessed thing to read an illuminated Bible lit up by the radiance of the Holy Ghost. Hast thou read the Bible and studied it, my brother, and yet have thine eyes been unenlightened? Go and say, "O Lord, gild the Bible for me. I want an expounded Bible. Illuminate it; shine upon it; for I cannot read it to profit, unless thou enlightenest me." Blind men may read the Bible with their fingers, but blind souls cannot. We want a light to read the Bible by, there is no reading it in the dark. Thus the Holy Spirit leads us into all truth, by suggesting ideas, by directing our thoughts, and by illuminating the Scriptures when we read them.

V. The last thing is *an evidence.*

The question arises, "How may I know whether I am enlightened by the Spirit's influence, and led into all truth?" First, you may know the Spirit's influence by its *unity*—he guides us into all *truth*: secondly, by its *universality*—he guides us into *all* truth.

First, if you are judging a minister, whether he has the Holy Ghost in him or not, you may know him in the first place, by *the constant unity of his testimony.* A man cannot be enlightened by the Holy Spirit, who preaches yea and nay. The Spirit never says one thing at one time and another thing at another time. There are indeed many good men who say both yea and nay, but still their contrary testimonies are not both from God the Spirit, for God the Spirit cannot witness to black and white, to a falsehood and truth. It has been always held as a first principle, that truth is one thing; but some persons say, "I find one thing in one part of the Bible and another thing in another, and though it contradicts itself I must believe it." All quite right, brother, if it did contradict itself; but the fault is not in the wood but in the carpenter. Many carpenters do not understand dovetailing—so there are many preachers who do not understand dovetailing. It is very nice work, and it is not easily learnt, it takes some apprenticeship to make all doctrines square together. Some preachers preach very good Calvinism for half-an-hour, and the next quarter-of-an hour, Arminianism.[2] If they are Calvinists, let them stick to it; if they are Arminians, let them stick to it, let their preaching be all of a piece. Don't let them pile up things, only to kick them all down again; let us have one thing woven from the top throughout, and let us not rend it. How did Solomon know the true mother of the child? "Cut it in halves," said he. The woman who was not the mother did not care, so long as the other did not get the whole, and she consented. "Ah," said the true

---

[2] Arminianism: a theology that rejects the Calvinist doctrines of predestination and election and believes that human free will is compatible with God's sovereignty. (*American Heritage Dictionary*, 4th Edtion, 2000.)

mother, "give her the living child. Let her have it, rather than cut it in halves." So the true child of God would say

> I give it up, let my opponent conquer; I do not want to have the truth cut in halves. I would rather be all wrong, than have the Word altered to my taste.

We do not want to have a divided Bible. No, we claim the whole living child, or none at all. We may rest assured of this, that until we get rid of our linsey-woolsey[3] doctrine, and cease to sow mingled seed, we shall not have a blessing. An enlightened mind cannot believe a gospel which denies itself; it must be one thing or the other. One thing cannot contradict another, and yet it and its opposite be equally true. You may know the Spirit's influence then, by the unity of its testimony.

And you may know it by its *universality*. The true child of God will not be led into *some* truth but into *all* truth. When first he starts, he will not know half the truth: he will believe it but not understand it; he will have the germ of it but not the sum total in all its breadth and length. There is nothing like learning by experience. A man cannot set up for a theologian in a week. Certain doctrines take years to develop themselves. Like the aloe that taketh a hundred years to be dressed, there be some truths that must lie long in the heart before they really come out and make themselves appear so that we can speak of them as that we do know; and testify of that which we have seen. The Spirit will gradually lead us into all truth. For instance if it be true that Jesus Christ is to reign upon the earth personally for a thousand years, as I am inclined to believe it is, if I be under the Spirit, that will be more and more opened to me, until I with confidence declare it. Some men begin very timidly. A man says, at first, "I know we are justified by faith, and have peace with God, but so many have cried out against eternal justification, that I am afraid of it." But he is gradually enlightened, and led to see that in the same hour when all his debts were paid, a full discharge was given; that in the moment when its sin was cancelled, every elect soul was justified in God's mind, though they were not; justified in their own minds till afterwards. The Spirit shall lead you into all truth.

Now, what are the practical inferences from this great doctrine? The first is with reference to the Christian who is afraid of his own ignorance. How many are there who are just enlightened and have tasted of heavenly things, who are afraid they are too ignorant to be saved! Beloved, God the Holy Spirit can teach anyone, however illiterate, however uninstructed. I have known some men who were almost idiots before conversion, but they afterwards had their faculties wonderfully developed. Some time ago there was a man who was so ignorant that he could not read, and he never spoke anything like grammar in his life, unless by mistake; and moreover, he was considered to be what the people in his neighborhood called "daft." But when he

---

[3] Linsey-woolsey: a coarse, blended fabric made of wool and cotton, or wool and linen.

was converted, the first thing he did was to pray. He stammered out a few words, and in a little time his powers of speaking began to develop themselves. Then he thought he would like to read the Scriptures, and after long, long months of labor, he learned to read; and what was the next thing? He thought he could preach; and he did preach a little in his own homely way, in his house. Then he thought "I must read a few more books." And so his mind expanded, until, I believe he is at the present day, a useful minister, settled in a country village, laboring for God. It needs but little intellect to be taught of God. If you feel your ignorance, do not despair. Go to the Spirit—the great Teacher—and ask his sacred influence, and it shall come to pass that he "shall guide you into all truth."

Another inference is this whenever any of our brethren do not understand the truth let us take a hint as to the best way of dealing with them. Do not let us controvert with them. I have heard many controversies, but never heard of any good from one of them. We have had controversies with certain men called Secularists, and very strong arguments have been brought against them; but I believe that the day of judgment shall declare that a very small amount of good was ever done by contending with these men. Better let them alone: where no fuel is, the fire goeth out; and he that debateth with them puts wood upon the fire. So with regard to Baptism. It is of no avail to quarrel with our Paedo-baptist[4] friends. If we simply pray for them that the God of truth may lead them to see the true doctrine, they will come to it far more easily than by discussions. Few men are taught by controversy, for

> A man convinced against his will,
> is of the same opinion still.

Pray for them that the Spirit of truth may lead them "into all truth." Do not be angry with your brother, but pray for him; cry, "Lord! open thou his eyes that he may behold wondrous things out of thy law."

Lastly, we speak to some of you who know nothing about the Spirit of truth, nor about the truth itself. It may be that some of you are saying, "We care not much which of you are right, we are happily indifferent to it." Ah! but, poor sinner, if thou knewest the gift of God, and who it was that spake the truth, thou wouldst not say, "I care not for it." If thou didst know how essential the truth is to thy salvation, thou wouldst not talk so. If thou didst know that the truth of God is—that thou art a worthless sinner, but if thou believest, then God from all eternity, apart from all thy merits, loved thee, and bought thee with the Redeemer's blood, and justified thee in the forum of Heaven, and will, by-and-by, justify thee in the forum of thy conscience through the Holy Ghost by faith; if thou didst know that there is

---

[4] Paedo-baptist: beliver in infant baptisim.

a Heaven for thee beyond the chance of a failure, a crown for thee, the lustre of which can never be dimmed—then thou wouldst say, "Indeed the truth is precious to my soul!" Why, my ungodly hearers, these men of error want to take away the truth, which alone can save you, the only gospel that can deliver you from Hell; they deny the great truths of free-grace, those fundamental doctrines which alone can snatch a sinner from Hell; and even though you do not feel interest in them now, I still would say, you ought to desire to see them promoted. May God give you to know the truth in your hearts! May the Spirit "guide you into all truth!" For if you do not know the truth here, recollect there will be a sorrowful learning of it in the dark chambers of the pit, where the only light shall be the flames of Hell! May you here know the truth! And the truth shall make you free: and if the Son shall make you free, you shall be free indeed, for he says, "I am the way, the truth, the life." Believe on Jesus, thou chief of sinners; trust his love and mercy, and thou art saved, for God the Spirit giveth faith and eternal life.

The Outpouring of the Holy Spirit

Delivered on Sabbath morning, June 20, 1858 at the Music Hall, Royal Surrey Gardens. No. 201.

While Peter yet spake these words, the Holy Ghost fell on all them which heard the Word.—Acts 10:44

The Bible is a book of the revelation of God. The God after whom the heathen blindly searched, and for whom reason gropes in darkness, is here plainly revealed to us in the pages of divine authorship, so that he who is willing to understand as much of Godhead as man can know, may here learn it if he be not willingly ignorant and willfully obstinate. The doctrine of the Trinity is specially taught in Holy Scripture. The word certainly does not occur, but the three divine persons of the One God are frequently and constantly mentioned, and Holy Scripture is exceedingly careful that we should all receive and believe that great truth of the Christian religion, that the Father is God, that the Son is God, that the Spirit is God, and yet there are not three Gods but one God: though they be each of them very God of very God, yet three in one and one in three is the Jehovah whom we worship. You will notice in the works of *creation* how carefully the Scriptures assure us that all the three divine persons took their share. "In the beginning Jehovah created the heavens and the earth;" and in another place we are told that God said "Let *us* make man"—not one person, but all three taking counsel with each other with regard to the making of mankind. We know that the Father hath laid the foundations and fixed those solid beams of light on which the blue arches of the sky are sustained; but we know with equal certainty that Jesus Christ, the eternal *Logos*, was with the Father in the beginning, and "without him was not anything made that was made:" moreover we have equal certainty that the Holy Spirit had a hand in Creation, for we are told that "the earth was without form and void, and darkness was upon the face of the earth; and the spirit of the Lord moved upon the face of the waters;" and brooding with his dove-like wing, he brought out of the egg of chaos this mighty thing, the fair round world. We have the like proof of the three persons in the Godhead in the matter of *salvation*. We know that God the Father gave his Son; we have abundant proof that God the Father chose his people from before the foundations of the world, that he did invent the plan of salvation, and hath always given his free, willing, and joyous consent to the salvation of his people. With regard to the share that the Son had in salvation, that is apparent enough to all. For us men and for our salvation he came down from Heaven; he was incarnate in a mortal body; he was crucified, dead, and buried; he descended into Hades; the third day he rose again from the dead; he ascended into Heaven; he sitteth at the right hand of God, where also he maketh intercession for us. As to the Holy Spirit, we have equally sure proof that the Spirit of God worketh in conversion; for everywhere we are said to be begotten of the Holy Spirit; continually it is declared, that unless a man be born again from above, he cannot see the kingdom of God; while all the virtues and the graces of Christianity are described as being the fruits of the Spirit, because the Holy Spirit doth from first to last work in us and carry out that which Jesus Christ hath beforehand worked for us in his great redemption, which also God the Father hath designed for us in his great predestinating scheme of salvation.

Now, it is to the work of the Holy Spirit that I shall this morning specially direct your attention; and I may as well mention the reason why I do so. It is this. We have received continually fresh confirmations of the good news from a far country, which has already made glad the hearts of many of God's people. In the United States of America there is certainly a great awakening. No sane man living there could think of denying it. There may be something of spurious excitement mixed up with it, but that good, lasting good, has been accomplished, no rational man can deny. Two hundred and fifty thousand persons—that is, a quarter of a million—profess to have been regenerated since December last; have made a profession of their faith; and have united themselves with different sections of God's church. The work still progresses, if anything, at a more rapid rate than before, and that which makes me believe the work to be genuine is just this—that the enemies of Christ's holy gospel are exceedingly wroth at it. When the devil roars at anything, you may rest assured there is some good in it. The devil is not like some dogs we know of; he never barks unless there is something to bark at. When Satan howls we may rest assured he is afraid his kingdom is in danger.

Now this great work in America has been manifestly caused by the outpouring of the Spirit, for no one minister has been a leader in it. All the ministers of the gospel have cooperated in it, but none of them have stood in the van[guard]. God himself has been the leader of his own hosts. It began with a desire for prayer. God's people began to pray; the prayer-meetings were better attended than before. It was then proposed to hold meetings at times that had never been set apart for prayer; these also were well attended; and now, in the city of Philadelphia, at the hour of noon, every day in the week, three thousand persons can always be seen assembled together for prayer in one place. Men of business, in the midst of their toil and labor, find an opportunity of running in there and offering a word of prayer, and then return to their occupations. And so, throughout all the States, prayer-meetings, larger or smaller in number, have been convened. And there has been real prayer. Sinners beyond all count have risen up in the prayer-meeting, and have requested the people of God to pray for them; thus making public to the world that they had a desire after Christ; they have been prayed for, and the church has seen that God verily doth hear and answer prayer. I find that the Unitarian ministers for a little while took no notice of it. Theodore Parker snarls and raves tremendously at it, but he is evidently in a maze; he does not understand the mystery, and acts with regard to it as swine are said to do with pearls. While the church was found asleep, and doing very little, the Socinian[1] could afford to stand in his pulpit and sneer at anything like evangelical religion, but now that there has been an awakening, he looks like a man that has just awakened out of sleep. He sees something; he does not know what it is. The power of religion is just that which will always puzzle the Unitarian, for he knows but little about that. At the form of religion he is not much amazed, for he can to an extent endorse that himself, but the supernaturalism of the gospel—the mystery—the miracle—the power—the demonstration of the Spirit that comes with the preaching, is what such men cannot comprehend, and they gaze and wonder, and then become filled with wrath, but still they have to confess there is something there they cannot understand, a mental phenomenon that is far beyond their philosophy—a thing which they cannot reach by all their science nor understand by all their reason.

Now, if we have the like effect produced in this land, the one thing we must seek is the outpouring of the Holy Spirit, and I thought, perhaps, this morning in preaching upon the work of the Holy Spirit, that text might be fulfilled—"Him that honoreth me I will honor." My sincere desire is to honor the Holy Spirit this morning, and if he will be pleased to honor his church in return, unto him shall be the glory forever.

"While Peter yet spake these words, the Holy Ghost fell on all them which heard the word." In the first place, I shall endeavor to describe *the method of the*

---

[1] Socinian: 16th century Unitarian sect that denied Jesus' divinity.

Spirit's operation, secondly, *the absolute necessity of the Holy Spirit's influence*, if we could see men converted, and then, in the third place, I shall suggest the ways and means by which under divine grace we may obtain a like falling down of the Spirit upon our churches.

I. In the first place, then, I will endeavor to explain *the method of the Holy Spirit's operations.*

But let me guard myself against being misunderstood. We can explain *what* the Spirit does, but *how* he does it, no man must pretend to know. The work of the Holy Spirit is the peculiar mystery of the Christian religion. Almost any other thing is plain, but this must remain an inscrutable secret into which it were wrong for us to attempt to pry. Who knoweth where the winds are begotten? Who knoweth, therefore, how the Spirit worketh, for he is like the wind?

> The wind bloweth where it listeth, and thou hearest the sound thereof but canst not tell whence it cometh, and whither it goeth: so is everyone that is born of the Spirit.

In Holy Scripture certain great secrets of nature are mentioned as being parallel with the secret working of the Spirit. The procreation of children is instanced as a parallel wonder, for we know not the mystery thereof; how much less, therefore, shall we expect to know that more secret and hidden mystery of the new birth and new creation of man in Christ Jesus. But let no man be staggered at this, for they are mysteries in nature: the wisest man will tell you there are depths in nature into which he cannot dive, and heights into which he cannot soar. He who pretends to have unraveled the knot of creation hath made a mistake, he may have cut the knot by his rough ignorance, and by his foolish conjectures, but the knot itself must remain beyond the power of man's unraveling, until God himself shall explain the secret. There are marvelous things, that, as yet, men have sought to know in vain. They may, perhaps, discover many of them, but how the Spirit works, no man can know. But now I wish to explain *what* the Holy Spirit does, although we cannot tell how he does it. I take it that the Holy Spirit's work in conversion is twofold. First it is an awakening of the powers that man already has, and secondly, it is an implantation of powers which he never had at all.

In the great work of the new birth, the Holy Spirit first of all *awakens the mental powers*; for be it remembered that the Holy Spirit never gives any man *new* mental powers. Take, for instance, reason—the Holy Spirit does not give men reason, for they have reason prior to their conversion. What the Holy Spirit does is to teach our reason, right reason—to set our reason in the right track, so that he can use it for the high purpose of discerning between good and evil; between the precious and vile. The Holy Spirit does not give man a will, for man has a will before; but he makes the will that was in bondage to Satan, free to the service of God. The Holy

Spirit gives no man the power to think, or the organ of belief—for man has power to believe or think, as far as the mental act is concerned; but he gives that belief which is already there, a tendency to believe the right thing, and he gives to the power of thought, the propensity to think in the right way, so that instead of thinking irregularly, we begin to think as God would have us think, and our mind desireth to walk in the steps of God's revealed truth. There may be here, this morning, a man of enlarged understanding in things political—but his understanding is darkened with regard to spiritual things—he sees no beauty in the person of Christ—he sees nothing desirable in the way of holiness—he chooses the evil and forsakes the good. Now the Holy Spirit will not give him a new understanding, but he will cleanse his old understanding so that he will discern between things that differ, and shall discover that it is but a poor thing to enjoy "the pleasures of sin for a season," and let go an "eternal weight of glory." There shall be a man here too who is desperately set against religion, and willeth not to come to God—and do what we will, we are not able to persuade him to change his mind and turn to God. The Holy Spirit will not make a new will in that man, but he will turn his old will, and instead of willing to do evil he will make him will to do right—he will make him will to be saved by Christ—he will make him "willing in the day of his power." Remember, there is no power in man so fallen but that the Holy Spirit can raise it up. However debased a man may be, in one instant, by the miraculous power of the Spirit, all his faculties may be cleansed and purged. Ill-judging reason may be made to judge rightly; stout, obstinate wills may be made to run willingly in the ways of God's commandments; evil and depraved affections may in an instant be turned to Christ, and old desires that are tainted with vice, may be replaced by heavenly aspirations.

The work of the Spirit on the mind is the re-modeling of it; the new forming of it. He doth not bring new material to the mind—it is in another part of the man that he puts up a new structure—but he puts the mind that had fallen out of order into its proper shape. He builds up pillars that had fallen down, and erects the palaces that had crumbled to the earth. This is the first work of the Holy Spirit upon the mind of man.

Besides this, the Holy Spirit gives to men *powers which they never had before*. According to Scripture, I believe man is constituted in a three-fold manner. He has a body; by the Holy Spirit that body is made the temple of the Lord. He has a mind; by the Holy Spirit that mind is made like an altar in the temple. But man by nature is nothing higher than that; he is mere body and soul. When the Spirit comes, he breathes into him a third higher principle which we call the spirit. The apostle describes man as man, "body, soul and spirit." Now if you search all the mental writers through, you will find they all declare there are only two parts—body and mind; and they are quite right, for they deal with unregenerate man; but in regenerate man there is a third principle as much superior to mere mind as mind is superior to dead animal matter. That third principle is that with which a man *prays*; it is that with which he lovingly believes; or rather it is that which compels the mind to perform these acts. It is that which, operating upon the mind, makes the same use of the mind as the mind does of the body. When, after desiring to walk, I make my legs move, it is my mind that compels them; and so my *spirit*, when I desire to pray, compels my mind to think the thought of prayer and compels my soul also, if I desire to praise, to think the thought of praise, and lift itself upward towards God. As the body without the soul is dead, so the soul without the spirit is dead, and one work of the spirit is to quicken the dead soul by breathing into it the firing Spirit. As it is written, "The first man, Adam, was made a living soul, but the second Adam was made a quickening *Spirit*"—and, "as we have borne the image of the earthly, so must we bear the image of the heavenly." That is, we must have in us, if we would be converted, the quickening spirit, which is put into us by God the Holy Ghost. I say again, the spirit has powers which the mind never has. It has the power of communion with Christ, which to a degree is a mental act, but it can no more be performed by man without the spirit, than the act of walking could be performed by man, if he were destitute of a soul to suggest the idea of walking. The spirit suggests the thoughts of communion which the mind obeys and carries out. Nay, there are times, I think, when the spirit leaves the mind altogether, times when we forget everything of earth and one almost ceases to think, to reason, to judge, to weigh, or to will. Our souls are like the chariots of Amminadib, drawn swiftly onwards without any powers of volition. We lean upon the breast of Jesus, and in rhapsody divine, and in ecstasy celestial, we enjoy the fruits of the land of the blessed, and pluck the clusters of Eschol before entering into the land of promise.

 I think I have clearly put these two points before you. The work of the Spirit consists, first, in awakening powers already possessed by man, but which were asleep and out of order; and in the next place in putting into man powers which he had not before. And to make this simple to the humblest mind, let me suppose man to be something like a machine; all the wheels are out of order, the cogs do not strike upon each other, the wheels do not turn regularly, the rods will not act, the order is gone. Now, the first work of the Spirit is to put these wheels in the right place, to fit the wheels upon the axles, to put the right axle to the right wheel, then to put wheel to wheel, so that they may act upon each other. But that is not all his work. The next thing is to put fire and steam so that these things shall go to work. He does not put fresh wheels, he puts old wheels into order, and then he puts the motive power which is to move the whole. First he puts our mental powers into their proper order and condition, and then he puts a living quickening spirit, so that all these shall move according to the holy will and law of God.

But, mark you, this is not all the Holy Spirit does. For if he were to do this, and then leave us, none of us would get to Heaven. If any of you should be so near to Heaven that you could hear the angels singing over the walls—if you could almost see within the pearly gates, still, if the Holy Spirit did not help you the last step, you would never enter there. All the work is through his divine operation. Hence it is the Spirit who keeps the wheels in motion, and who tales away that defilement which, naturally engendered by our original sin, falls upon the machine and puts it out of order. He takes this away, and keeps the machine constantly going without injury, until at last he removes man from the place of defilement to the land of the blessed, a perfect creature, as perfect as he was when he came from the mold of his Maker.

And I must say, before I leave this point, that all the former part of what I have mentioned is done instantaneously. When a man is converted to God, it is done in a moment. Regeneration is an instantaneous work. Conversion to God, the fruit of regeneration, occupies all our life, but regeneration itself is effected in an instant. A man hates God; the Holy Spirit makes him love God. A man is opposed to Christ, he hates his gospel, does not understand it and will not receive it: the Holy Spirit comes, puts light into his darkened understanding, takes the chain from his bandaged will, gives liberty to his conscience, gives life to his dead soul, so that the voice of conscience is heard, and the man becomes a new creature in Christ Jesus. And all this is done, mark you, by the instantaneous supernatural influence of God the Holy Ghost working as he willeth among the sons of men.

II. Having thus dwelt upon the method of the Holy Spirit's work, I shall now turn to the second point, *the absolute necessity of the Spirit's work in order to conversion.*

In our text we are told that "while Peter spake these words, the Holy Ghost fell on all them which heard the word." Beloved, the Holy Ghost fell on Peter first, or else it would not have fallen on his hearers. There is a necessity that the preacher himself, if we are to have souls saved, should be under the influence of the Spirit. I have constantly made it my prayer that I might be guided by the Spirit even in the smallest and least important parts of the service; for you cannot tell but that the salvation of a soul may depend upon the reading of a hymn, or upon the selection of a chapter. Two persons have joined our church and made a profession of being converted simply through my reading a hymn—

Jesus, lover of my soul

They did not remember anything else in the hymn, but those words made such a deep impression upon their mind, that they could not help repeating them for days afterwards, and then the thought arose, "Do I love Jesus?" And then they considered what strange ingratitude it was that he should be the lover of their souls, and yet they should not love him. Now I believe the Holy Spirit led me to read that hymn. And many persons have been converted by some striking saying of the preacher. But why was it the preacher uttered that saying? Simply because he was led thereunto by the Holy Spirit. Rest assured, beloved, that when any part of the sermon is blessed to your heart, the minister said it because he was ordered to say it by his Master. I might preach today a sermon which I preached on Friday, and which was useful then, and there might be no good whatever come from it now, because it might not be the sermon which the Holy Ghost would have delivered today. But if with sincerity of heart I have sought God's guidance in selecting the topic, and he rests upon me in the preaching of the Word, there is no fear but that it shall be found adapted to your immediate wants. The Holy Spirit must rest upon your preachers. Let them have all the learning of the wisest men, and all the eloquence of such men as Desmosthenes and Cicero, still the Word cannot be blessed to you, unless first of all the Spirit of God hath guided the minister's mind in the selection of his subject, and in the discussion of it.

But if Peter himself were under the hand of the Spirit, that would fail unless the Spirit of God, then, did fall upon our hearers; and I shall endeavor now to show the absolute necessity of the Spirit's work in the conversion of men.

Let us remember what kind of thing the work is, and we shall see that other means are altogether out of the question. It is quite certain that men cannot be converted by physical means. The Church of Rome thought that she could convert men by means of armies; so she invaded countries, and threatened them with war and bloodshed unless they would repent and embrace her religion. However, it availed but little, and men were prepared to die rather than leave their faith. She therefore tried those beautiful things—stakes, racks, dungeons, axes, swords, fire; and by these things she hoped to convert men. You have heard of the man who tried to wind up his watch with a pick-axe. That man was extremely wise, compared with the man who thought to touch mind through matter. All the machines you like to invent cannot touch mind. Talk about tying angel's wings with green withes [reeds], or manacling the cherubim with iron chains, and then talk about meddling with the minds of men through physical means. Why, the things don't set; they cannot act. All the king's armies that ever were, and all the warriors clothed with mail, with all their ammunition, could never touch the mind of man. That is an impregnable castle which is not to be reached by physical agency.

Nor, again, can man be converted by moral argument. "Well," says one, "I think he may. Let a minister preach earnestly, and he may persuade men to be converted." Ah! beloved, it is for want of knowing better that you say so. Melancthon thought so, but you know what he said after he tried it—"Old Adam is too strong for young Melancthon." So will every preacher find it, if he thinks his arguments can ever convert man. Let me give you a parallel case. Where is the logic that can persuade an Ethiopian to change his skin? By what argument can you induce a leopard to renounce his spots? Even so may he that is accustomed to do evil, learn to do well. But if the Ethiopian's skin be changed it must be by a supernatural process, and if the leopard's spots be removed, he that made the leopard must do it. Even so is it with the heart of man. If sin were a thing *ab extra* and external, we could induce man to change it. For instance, you may induce a man to leave off drunkenness or swearing, because those things are not a part of his nature—he has added that vice to his original depravity. But the hidden evil at the heart is beyond all moralsuasion. I dare say a man might have enough argument to induce him to hang himself, but I am certain no argument will ever induce him to hang his sins, to hang his self-righteousness, and to come and humble himself at the foot of the cross; for the religion of Christ is so contrary to all the propensities of man, that it is like swimming against the stream to approach it, for the stream of man's will and man's desire is exactly the opposite of the religion of Jesus Christ. If you wanted a proof of that, at the lifting of my finger, there are thousands in this hall who would rise to prove it, for they would say,

> I have found it so, sir, in my experience; I hated religion as much as any men; I despised Christ, and his people, and I know not to this day how it is that I am what I am, unless it be the work of God.

I have seen the tears run down a man's cheeks when he has come to me in order to be united to the church of Christ, and he has said,

> Sir, I wonder how it is I am here today. If anyone had told me a year ago that I should think as I now think, and feel as I now feel, I should have called him a born fool for his pains. I used to say I never would be one of those canting Methodists, I liked to spend my Sunday in pleasure, and I did not see why I was to be cooping myself up in the house of God listening to a man talk. I pray, sire—no, not I! I said the best providence in all the world was a good strong pair of hands, and to take care of what you got. If any man talked to me about religion, why I would slam the door in his face, and pretty soon put him out; but the things that I loved then, I now hate, and the things that then I hated, now I love. I cannot do or say enough to show how total is the change that has been wrought in me. It must have been the work of God; it could not have been wrought by me, I feel assured; it must be someone greater than myself, who could thus turn my heart.

I think these two things are proofs that we want something more than nature, and since physical agency will not do, and mere moral suasion will never accomplish it, that there must be an absolute necessity for the Holy Spirit.

But again, if you will just think a minute what the work is, you will soon see that none but God can accomplish it. In the Holy Scripture, conversion is often spoken of as being a new creation. If you talk about creating yourselves, I should feel obliged if you would create a fly first. Create a gnat; create a grain of sand; and when you have created that, you may talk about creating a new heart. Both are alike impossible, for creation is the work of God. But still, if you could create a grain of dust, or create even a world, it would not be half the miracle, for you must first find a thing which has created itself. Could that be? Suppose you had no existence, how could you create yourself? Nothing cannot produce anything. Now, how can man re-create himself? A man cannot create himself into a new condition, when he has no being in that condition, but is, as yet, a thing that is not.

Then, again, the work of creation is said to be like the resurrection. "We are alive from the dead." Now, can the dead in the grave raise themselves? Let any minister who thinks he can convert souls, go and raise a corpse. Let him go and stand in one of the cemeteries, and bid the tombs open wide their mouths, and make room for those once buried there to awaken—and he will have to preach in vain. But if he could do it, that is not the miracle: it is for the dead to raise themselves, for an inanimate corpse to kindle in its own breast the spark of life anew. If the work be a resurrection, a creation, does it not strike you that it must be beyond the power of man? It must be wrought in him by no one less than God himself.

And there is yet one more consideration, and I shall have concluded this point. Beloved, even if man could save himself, I would have you recollect how averse he is to it. If we could make our hearers all willing, the battle would be accomplished. "Well," says one, "If I am willing to be saved, can I not be saved?" Assuredly you can, but the difficulty is, we cannot bring men to be willing. That shows, therefore, that there must be a constraint put upon their will. There must be an influence exerted upon them, which they have not in themselves, in order to make them willing in the day of God's power. And this is the glory of the Christian religion. The Christian religion has within its own bowels [insides] power to spread itself. We do not ask you to be willing first. We come and tell you the news, and we believe that the Spirit of God, working with us, will make you willing. If the progress of the Christian religion depended upon the voluntary assent of mankind, it would never go an inch further. But because the Christian religion has within an omnipotent influence, constraining men to believe it, it is therefore that it is, and must be, triumphant, "till like a sea of glory it spreads from shore to shore."

III. Now I shall conclude by bringing one or two thoughts forward, with regard to *what must be done at this time in order to bring down the Holy Spirit.*

It is quite certain, beloved, if the Holy Spirit willed to do it, that every man, woman, and child in this place might be converted now. If God, the Sovereign Judge of all, would be pleased now to send out his Spirit, every inhabitant of this million-peopled city might be brought at once to turn unto the living God. Without instrumentality, without the preacher, without books, without anything—God has it in his power to convert men. We have known persons about their business, not thinking about religion at all, who have had a thought injected into their heart, and that thought has been the prolific mother of a thousand meditations. and through these meditations they have been brought to Christ. Without the aid of the minister, the Holy Spirit has thus worked, and today he is not restrained. There may be some men, great in infidelity, staunch in opposition to the cross of Christ—but, without asking their consent, the Holy Spirit can pull down the strong man, and make the mighty man bow himself.

For when we talk of the Omnipotent God, there is nothing too great for him to do. But, beloved, God has been pleased to put great honor upon instrumentality; he could work without it if he pleased, but he does not do so. However, this is the first thought I want to give you; *if you would have the Holy Spirit exert himself in our midst, you must first of all look to him and not to instrumentality.* When Jesus Christ preached, there were very few converted under him, and the reason was, because the Holy Spirit was not abundantly poured forth. He had the Holy Spirit without measure himself, but on others the Holy Spirit was not as yet poured out. Jesus Christ said, "Greater works than these shall ye do, because I go to my Father, in order to send the Holy Spirit;" and recollect that those few who were converted under Christ's ministry, were not converted by him, but by the Holy Spirit that rested upon him at that time. Jesus of Nazareth was anointed of the Holy Spirit. Now then, if Jesus Christ, the great founder of our religion, needed to be anointed of the Holy Spirit, how much more our ministers? And if God would always make the distinction even between his own Son as an instrument, and the Holy Spirit as the agent, how much more ought we to be careful to do that between poor puny men and the Holy Spirit? Never let us hear you say again, "So many persons were converted by So-and so." They were not. If converted, they were not converted by man. Instrumentality is to be used, but the Spirit is to have the honor of it. Pay no more a superstitious reverence to man, think no more that God is tied to your plans, and to your agencies. Do not imagine that so many city missionaries [means] so much good will be done. Do not say, "So many preachers, so many sermons, so many souls saved." Do not say, "So many Bibles, so many tracts, so much good done." Not so: use these, but remember it is not in that proportion the blessing comes; it is: *"So much Holy Spirit, so many souls in-gathered."*

And now another thought. If we would have the Spirit, beloved, we must each of us try to honor him. There are some chapels into which, if you were to enter, you would never know there was a Holy Spirit. Mary Magdalene said of old, "They have taken away my Lord, and I know not where they have laid him," and the Christian might often say so, for there is nothing said about the Lord until they come to the end, and then there is just the benediction, or else you would not know that there were three persons in one God at all. Until our churches honor the Holy Spirit, we shall never see it abundantly manifested in our midst. Let the preacher always confess before he preaches that he relies upon the Holy Spirit. Let him burn his manuscript and depend upon the Holy Spirit. If the Spirit does not come to help him, let him be still and let the people go home and pray that the Spirit will help him next Sunday.

And do you also, in the use of all your agencies, always honor the Spirit? We often begin our religious meetings without prayer; it is all wrong. We must honor the Spirit; unless we put him first, he will never make crowns for us to wear. He will get victories, but he will have the honor of them, and if we do not give to him the honor, he will never give to us the privilege and success. And best of all, if you would have the Holy Spirit, let us meet together earnestly to pray for him. Remember, the Holy Spirit will not come to us as a church, unless we seek him. "For this thing will I be enquired of by the house of Israel to do it for them." We purpose during the coming week to hold meetings of special prayer, to supplicate for a revival of religion. On the Friday morning I opened the first prayer meeting at Trinity Chapel, Brixton; and, I think, at seven o'clock, we had as many as two hundred and fifty persons gathered together. It was a pleasant sight. During the hour, nine brethren prayed, one after the other; and I am sure there was the spirit of prayer there. Some persons present sent up their names, asking that we would offer special petitions for them; and I doubt not the prayers will be answered. At Park Street, on Monday morning, we shall have a prayer-meeting from eight to nine; then during the rest of the week there will be a prayer-meeting in the morning from seven to eight. On Monday evening we shall have the usual prayer-meeting at seven, when I hope there will be a large number attending. I find that my brother, Baptist Noel, has commenced morning and evening prayer-meetings, and they have done the same thing in Norwich and many provincial towns, where, without any pressure, the people are found willing to come.

I certainly did not expect to see so many as two hundred and fifty persons at an early hour in the morning meet together for prayer. I believe it was a good sign. The Lord hath put prayer into their hearts and therefore they were willing to come, "Prove me now here, saith the Lord of hosts, and see if I do not pour you out a blessing so that there shall not be room enough to receive it." Let us meet and pray, and if God doth not hear us, it will be the first time he has broken his promise. Come, let us go up to the sanctuary; let us meet together in the house of the Lord, and offer solemn supplication; and I say again, if the Lord doth not make bare his arm in the sight of all the people, it will be the reverse of all his previous actions, it will be the contrary of all his promises, and contradictory to himself. We have only to try him, and the result is certain. In dependence on his Spirit, if we only meet for prayer, the Lord shall bless us, and all the ends of the earth shall fear him. O Lord, lift up thyself because of thine enemies; pluck thy right hand out of thy bosom, O Lord our God, for Christ's sake, Amen.

The Holy Spirit Compared to the Wind

Preached at the Metropolitan Tabernacle, Newington. Published 1865. No. 630.

The wind bloweth where it listeth, and thou hearest the sound thereof, but canst not tell whence it cometh, and whither it goeth: so is everyone that is born of the Spirit.—John 3:8

At the present moment, I am not able to enter fully into the subject of the new birth. I am very weary, both in body and mind, and cannot attempt that great and mysterious theme. To everything there is a season and a time for every purpose under Heaven, and it is not the time to preach upon regeneration when the head is aching, nor to discourse upon the new nature when the mind is distracted. I selected my text with the intention of fixing upon one great illustration, which strikes me just now as being so suggestive, that with divine assistance, I may be able to work it out with profit to you, and ease to myself. I shall endeavor to bring before you the parallel which our Savior here draws, between the wind and the Holy Spirit. It is a remarkable fact, known I dare say to most of you, that both in the Hebrew and Greek languages the same word is used for spirit and for wind, so that our Savior as it were rode upon the wings of the wind, while he was instructing the seeking Rabbi in the deep things of God; he caught at the very name of the wind, as a means of fastening a spiritual truth upon the memory of the enquirer, hinting to us that language should be watched by the teacher, that he may find out suitable words, and employ those which will best assist the disciple to comprehend and to retain his teaching. "The wind," said he, "bloweth," and the very same word would have been employed if he had meant to say, "The Spirit bloweth where he listeth." There was intended, doubtless, to be a very close and intimate parallel between the Spirit of God and the wind, or otherwise the great ruler of providence, who invisibly controlled the confusion of Babel, would not have fashioned human language so that the same word should stand for both. Language, as well as nature, illustrates the wisdom of God.

It is only in *his* light that we see light: may the Holy Spirit be graciously pleased to reveal himself in his divine operations to all our waiting minds. We are taught in God's Word that the Holy Spirit comes upon the sons of men, and makes them new creatures. Until he enters them, they are "dead in trespasses and sins." They cannot discern the things of God, because divine truths are spiritual and spiritually discerned, and unrenewed men are carnal, and possess not the power to search out the deep things of God. The Spirit of God new-creates the children of God, and then in their new-born spirituality, they discover and come to understand spiritual things, but not before; and, therefore, my beloved hearers, unless you *possess* the Spirit, no metaphors, however simple, can reveal him to you. Let us not mention the name of the Holy Spirit without due honor. Forever blessed be thou, most glorious Spirit, co-equal and co-eternal with the Father and with the Son; let all the angels of God worship thee! Be thou had in honor, world without end!

I. We will consider *in what sense the Holy Ghost may be compared to the wind*.

The Spirit of God, to help the spiritually minded in their study of his character and nature condescends to compare himself to dew, fire, oil, water, and other suggestive types; and among the rest, our Savior uses the metaphor of wind. What was the first thought here but that of *mystery*? It was the objection on the score of mystery which our Lord was trying to remove from the mind of Nicodemus. Nicodemus in effect said,

> I cannot understand it; how can it be? A man born again when he is old, created over again, and that from an invisible agency from above? How can these things be?

Jesus at once directed his attention to the wind, which is none the less real and operative because of its mysterious origin and operation. You cannot tell whence the wind cometh: you know it blows from the north or from the west, but at what particular place does that wind start on its career? Where will it pause in its onward flight? You see that it is blowing to the east or to the west, but where is its halting-place? Whence came these particles of air which rush so rapidly past? Whither are they going? By what law are they guided in their course, and where will their journey end? The gale may be blowing due east here, but it may be driving west a hundred miles away. In one district the wind may be rushing from the north, and yet not far from it there may be a strong current from the south. Those who ascend in balloons tell us that they meet with cross currents; one wind blowing in this direction, and another layer of air moving towards an opposite quarter; how is this? If you have watched the skies, you must occasionally have noticed a stream of clouds hurrying to the right, while higher up, another company is sailing to the left. It is a question whether thunder and lightning may not be produced by the friction of two currents of air traveling in different directions; but why is it that this current takes it into its head to go this way, while another steers for quite another point? Will they meet across each other's path in regions far away? Are there whirlpools in the air as in the water? Are these eddies, currents, rivers of air, lakes of air? Is the whole atmosphere like the sea, only composed of less dense matter? If so, what is it that stirs up that great deep of air, and bids it howl in the hurricane, and then constrains it to subside into the calm?

The philosopher may scheme some conjecture to prove that the "trade winds" blow at certain intervals because of the sun crossing the equator at those periods, and that there must necessarily be a current of air going towards the equator because of the rarefaction; but he cannot tell you why the weathercock on yonder church steeple turned this morning from south-west to due east. He cannot tell me why it is that the sailor finds that his sails are at one time filled with wind, and in a few minutes they fall loosely about, so that he must steer upon another tack if he would make headway. The various motions of the air remain a mystery to all but the infinite Jehovah. My brethren, the like mystery is observed in the work of the Spirit of God. His person and work are not to be comprehended by the mind of man. He may be here tonight, but you cannot see him: he speaks to one heart, but others cannot hear his voice. He is not recognizable by the unrefined senses of the unregenerate. The spiritual man discerns him, feels him, hears him, and delights in him, but neither wit nor learning can lead a man into the secret. The believer is often bowed down with the weight of the Spirit's glory, or lifted up upon the wings of his majesty; but even he knows not how these feelings are wrought in him. The fire of holy life is at seasons gently fanned with the soft breath of divine comfort, or the deep sea of spiritual existence stirred with the mighty blast of the Spirit's rebuke; but still it is evermore a mystery how the eternal God comes into contact with the finite mind of his creature man, filling all heaven meanwhile, and yet dwelling in a human body as in a temple—occupying all space, and yet operating upon the will, the judgment, the mind of the poor insignificant creature called man. We may enquire, but who can answer us? We may search, but who shall lead us into the hidden things of the Most High? He brooded over chaos and produced order, but who shall tell us after what fashion he wrought? He overshadowed the Virgin and prepared a body for the Son of God, but into this secret who shall dare to pry? His is the anointing, sealing, comforting, and sanctifying of the saints, but how worketh he all these things? He maketh intercession for us according to the will of God, he dwelleth in us and leadeth us into all truth, but who among us can explain to his fellow the order of the divine working? Though veiled from human eye like the glory which shone between the cherubim, we believe in the Holy Ghost, and therefore see him; but if our faith needed sight to sustain it, we should never believe at all.

Mystery is far from being all which the Savior would teach by this simile. Surely he meant to show us that the operations of the Spirit are like the wind for *divinity*. Who can create a wind? The most ambitious of human princes would scarcely attempt to turn, much less to send forth the wind. These steeds of the storm know no bit nor bridle, neither will they come at any man's bidding. Let our senators do what they will, they will scarcely have the madness to legislate for winds. Old Boreas, as the heathens called him, is not to be bound with chains and welded on earthly anvil, or in vulcanian forge. "The wind bloweth where it listeth;" and it does so because God directeth it and suffereth it not to stay for man, nor to tarry for the sons of men. So with the Spirit of God. All the true operations of the Spirit are due in no sense whatever to man, but always to God and to his sovereign will. Revivalists may get up excitement with the best intentions, and may warm peoples' hearts till they begin to cry out, but all this ends in nothing unless it is divine work. Have I not said scores of times in this pulpit, "All that is of nature's spinning, must be unraveled?" Every particle which nature puts upon the foundation will turn out to be but "wood, hay, and stubble," and will be consumed. It is only "the gold, the silver, and the precious stones" of God's building that will stand the fiery test. "Ye must be born again from above," for human regenerations are a lie. Thou mayest blow with thy mouth and produce some trifling effects upon trifles as light as air; man in his zeal may set the windmills of silly minds in motion; but, truly, to stir men's hearts with substantial and eternal verities [truths], needs a celestial breeze, such as the Lord alone can send.

Did not our Lord also intend to hint at the *sovereignty* of the Spirit's work? For what other reason did he say, "The wind bloweth where it listeth?" There is an arbitrariness about the wind, it does just as it pleases, and the laws which regulate its changes are to man unknown. "Free as the wind," we say—"the wild winds." So is the mighty working of God. It is a very solemn thought, and one which should tend to make us humble before the Lord—that we are, as to the matter of salvation, entirely in his hand! If I have a moth in my hand tonight, I can bruise its wings, or I can crush it at my will, and by no attempts of its own can it escape from me. And every sinner is absolutely in the hand of God, and, let him recollect, he is in the hand of an angry God, too.[1] The only comfort is, that he is in the hand of a God who for Jesus' sake, delights to have mercy upon even the vilest of the vile.

Sinner, God can give thee the Holy Spirit if he wills; but if he should say, "Let him alone," thy fate is sealed; thy damnation is sure. It is a thought which some

---

[1] This is a reference to Jonathan Edwards' 1741 sermon, "Sinners in the Hand of an Angry God," one of the most famous "fire and brimstone" sermons ever preached.

would say is "enough to freeze all energy." Beloved, I would to God it would freeze the energy of the flesh, and make the flesh stick dead in the sense of powerlessness; for God never truly begins to show his might till we have seen an end of all human power. I tell thee, sinner, thou art as dead concerning spiritual things as the corpse that is laid in its coffin, nay, as the corpse that is rotting in its grave, and has become like Lazarus in the tomb, stinking and offensive. There is a voice that can call thee forth out of thy sepulcher, but if that voice come not, remember where thou art—justly damned, justly ruined, justly cut off forever from all hope. What sayest thou? Dost thou tremble at this? Dost thou cry, "O God! have pity upon me?" He will hear thy cry, sinner, for there never yet was a sincere cry that went up to Heaven, though it were never so feeble, but what it had an answer of peace. When one of the old saints lay dying, he could only say, "O Lord, I trust thee *languida fide*"—with a languid faith. It is poor work that, but, oh! it is safe work. You can only trust Christ with a feeble faith; if it is such a poor trembling faith that it does not grip him, but only touches the hem of his garment, it nevertheless saves you. If you can look at him, though it be only a great way off, yet it saves you. And, oh what a comfort this is, that you are still on pleading terms with him and in a place of hope. "Whosoever believeth is not condemned." But, oh, do not trifle with the day of grace, lest having frequently heard the warning, and hardened thy neck just as often, thou shouldest "suddenly be destroyed, and that without remedy;" for if he shut out, none can bid thee come in; if he do but put to the iron bar, thou art shut out in the darkness of obstinacy, obduracy, and despair forever, the victim of thine own delusions. Sinner, if God save thee; he shall have all the glory, for he hath a right to do as he will, for he says, "I will have mercy on whom I will have mercy, and I will have compassion on whom I will have compassion."

But still I think I have not yet brought out what is in the text. Do you not think that the text was intended to show the *varied methods* in which the Spirit of God works in the conversion and regeneration of men? "The wind bloweth where it listeth [pleases]." Now, observe the different *force* of the wind. This afternoon, the wind seemed as if it would tear up every tree, and doubtless, had they been in leaf, many of those noble princes of the forest must have stretched themselves prone upon the earth; but God takes care that in these times of boisterous gales there should be no leaf, and therefore the wind gets but little purchase with which to drag up a tree. But the wind does not always blow as it did this afternoon. On a summer's evening there is such a gentle zephyr that even the gnats who have been arranging a dance among themselves are not disturbed, but keep to their proper places. Yea, the aspen seems as if it could be quiet, though you know it keeps forever quivering. According to the old legend, it was the tree on which the Savior hung, and therefore trembles still as though through fear of the sin which came upon it. 'Tis but a legend. There are times when all is still and calm, when everything is quiet, and you can scarcely detect the wind at all. Now, just so it is with the Spirit of God. To some of us he came like a "rushing mighty wind." Oh, what tearings of soul there were then! My spirit was like a sea tossed up into tremendous waves; made, as Job says, "To boil like a pot," till one would think the deep were hoary[2]. Oh, how that wind came crashing through my soul, and every hope I had was bowed as the trees of the wood in the tempest. Read the story of John Bunyan's conversion: it was just the same. Turn to Martin Luther: you find his conversion of the same sort. So might I mention hundreds of biographies in which the Spirit of God came like a tornado sweeping everything before it, and the men could not but feel that God was in the whirlwind.

To others he comes so gently, they cannot tell when first the Spirit of God came. They recollect that night when mother prayed so with brothers and sisters, and when they could not sleep for hours, because the big tears stood in their eyes on account of sin. They recollect the Sunday-school and the teacher there. They remember that earnest minister. They cannot say exactly when they gave their hearts to God, and they cannot tell about any violent convictions. They are often comforted by that text, "One thing I know, whereas I was blind, now I see;" but they cannot get any farther: they sometimes wish they could. Well, they need not wish it, for the Spirit of God, as a sovereign, will always choose his own way of operation; and if it be but the wind of the Holy Spirit, recollect it is as saving in its gentleness as in its terror, and is as efficient to make us new creatures when it comes with the zephyr's breath as when it comes with the hurricane's force. Do not quarrel with God's way of saving you. If you are brought to the cross, be thankful for it: Christ will not mind how you got there. If you can say "He is all my salvation, and all my desire," you never came to that without the Spirit of God bringing you to it. Do not therefore think you came the wrong way, for that is impossible.

Again, the wind not only differs in force, but it differs in *direction*. We have been saying several times the wind is always shifting. Perhaps there never were two winds that did blow exactly in the same direction. I mean that if we had power to detect the minute points of the compass, there would be found some deviation in every current, although, of course, for all practical purposes, it blows from certain distinct points which the mariner marks out. Now, the Spirit of God comes from different directions. You know very well, dear friends, that sometimes the Spirit of God will blow with mighty force from one denomination of Christians; then on a sudden they seem to be left, and another body of Christians God will raise up, fill with himself, and qualify for usefulness. In the days of [Charles] Wesley and [George] Whitefield, there was very little of the divine Spirit anywhere, except among the Methodists. I am sure they have not a monopoly of him now, the divine Spirit blows also from other quarters. Sometimes he uses one man, sometimes another. We hear of a revival in the North of Ireland, by-and-by it is in the

---

[2] Hoary: grey or white, as with age; ancient.

South of Scotland. It comes just as God wills, for direction; and you know, too, dear friends, it comes through different instrumentalities in the same church. Sometimes the wind blows from this pulpit: God blesses me to your conversion. Another time it is from my good sister, Mrs. Bartlett's class; on a third occasion it is the Sunday-school; again, it may be another class, or the preaching of the young men, or from the individual exertion of private believers. God causes that wind to blow just which way he wills.

He works also through different texts of Scripture. *You* were converted and blessed under one text: it was quite another that was made useful to *me*. Some of you were brought to Christ by terrors, others of you by love, by sweet wooing words. The wind blows as God directs. Now, dear friends, whenever you take up a religious biography, do not sit down and say, "Now I will see whether I am just like this person." Nonsense! God never repeats himself. Men make steel pens—thousands of grosses of them—all alike, but I will be bound to say that in quills from the common, there are no two of them precisely the same. If you look, you will soon discover that they differ in a variety of ways.

Certain gardeners cut their trees into the shape of cheeses and a number of unnatural forms, but God's trees do not grow that way, they grow just anyhow—gnarl their roots and twist their branches. Great painters do not continually paint the same picture again, and again, and again, and my Divine Master never puts his pencil on the canvas to produce the same picture twice. Every Christian is a distinct work of grace on God's part, which has in it some originality, some portion distinct from all others. I do not believe in trying to make all history uniform. It is said that Richard III had a hump-back. Whether he really was deformed, or whether history gave him the hump-back, I cannot tell, but it is said, that all his courtiers thought it was the most beautiful hump-back that ever was seen, and they all began to grow hump-backs too; and I have known ministers who had some peculiar idiosyncrasy of experience which was nothing better than a spiritual hump-back; but their people all began to have hump-backs too—to think and talk all in the same way, and to have the same doubts and fears. Now that will not do. It is not the way in which the Most High acts with regard to the wind, and if he chooses to take all the points of the compass, and make use of them all, let us bless and glorify his name.

Are not the different winds *various in their qualities?* Few of us like an east wind. Most of us are very glad when the wind blows from the south. Vegetation seems to love much the southwest. A stiff north-easter is enough to make us perish; and long continuance of the north, may well freeze the whole earth; while from the west, the wind seems to come laden with health from the deep blue sea; and though sometimes too strong for the sick, yet it is never a bad time when the west wind blows. The ancients all had their different opinions about wind; some were dry, some were rainy, some affected this disease, some touched this part of men, some the other. Certain it is that God's Holy Spirit has different qualities. In the Canticles [Song of Solomon] he blows softly with the sweet breath of love turn on farther, and you get that same Spirit blowing fiercely with threatening and denunciation; sometimes you find him convincing the world "of sin, of righteousness, of judgment," that is the north wind; at other times opening up Christ to the sinner, and giving him joy and comfort; that is the south wind, that blows softly, and gives a balminess in which poor troubled hearts rejoice; and yet "all these worketh the self-same Spirit."

Indeed, my subject is all but endless, and therefore I must stay. But even in the matter of *duration,* you know how the wind will sometimes blow six weeks in this direction, and, again, continue in another direction. And the Spirit of God does not always work with us: he does as he pleases; he comes, and he goes. We may be in a happy hallowed frame at one time, and at another we may have to cry, "Come from the four winds, O breath!"

II. We will consider in the second place, *the parallel between the Holy Spirit and the effects of the wind.*

"Thou hearest the sound thereof." Ah, that we do! The wind sometimes wails as if you could hear the cry of mariners far out at sea, or the moanings of the widows that must weep for them. And, oh! the Spirit of God sets men wailing with an exceeding bitter cry for sin, as one that is in sorrow for his first-born, "Thou hearest the sound thereof." Oh, it is a blessed sound, that wailing! Angels rejoice over "one sinner that repenteth." Then comes the wind at another time with a triumphant sound, and if there be an Aeolian [wind] harp in the window, how it swells, sweeps, descends, then rises again, gives all the tones of music, and makes glad the air with its jubilant notes. So with the Holy Spirit; sometimes he gives us faith, makes us bold, full of assurance, confidence, joy and peace in believing. "Thou hearest the sound" of a full diapason [full harmonious sound] of the Holy Spirit's mighty melody within the soul of man, filling him with peace and joy, and rest, and love. Sometimes the wind comes, too, with another sound, as though it were contending. You heard it, perhaps, this afternoon. We who are a little in the country hear it more than you do: it is as though giants were struggling in the sky together. It seems as if two seas of air—both lashed to fury—met, and dashed against some unseen cliffs with terrible uproar. The Spirit of God comes into the soul sometimes, and makes great contention with the flesh. Oh, what a stern striving there is against unbelief, against lust, against pride, against every evil thing.

"Thou hearest the sound thereof." Thou that knowest what divine experience means, thou knowest when to go forth to fight thy sins. When thou canst hear "the sound of a going in the tops of the mulberry trees," then thou dost bestir thyself to smite thy sins. Sometimes the wind comes with a sweep as though it were going on forever. It came past, and dashed through the trees, sweeping away the rotten branches, then away across the Alps, dashing down an avalanche in its course, still onward; and as it flew, it bore away everything that was frail and weak, and on, on, on it sped its way to some unknown goal. And thus it is sometimes the Spirit of God will come right through us, as if he were bearing us away to that spiritual heritage which is our sure future destiny—bearing away coldness, barrenness, everything before it. We do not lament then that we do not pray, we do not believe that we cannot pray; but "I can do everything," is our joyful shout as we are carried on the wings of the wind. "Thou hearest the sound thereof." I hope you have heard it sometimes in all its powerful, overwhelming, mighty influence, till your soul has been blown away. "Thou hearest the sound thereof."

But then the wind does something more than make a sound; and so does the Holy Spirit. It *works* and produces manifest results. Just think what the wind is doing tonight. I cannot tell at what pitch it may be now. It is just possible that in some part of the ocean a vessel scuds along almost under bare poles; the mariners do their best to reef the sails: away she goes: now the mast is gone: they do their best to bear up, but they find that in the teeth of the gale they cannot stand; the ship dashes on the rocks, and she is wrecked.

And, oh! the Spirit of God is a *great wrecker* of false hopes and carnal confidences. I have seen the Spirit of God come to a sinner like a storm to a ship at sea. He had to take down the top-gallants of his pride, and then every thread of carnal confidence had to be reefed, and then his hope itself had to be cut away; and on, on the vessel went, until she struck a rock, and down she went. The man from that time never dared trust in his merits, for he had seen his merits wrecked and broken in pieces by the wind.

The wind, too, recollect, is a *great leveler*. It always aims at everything that is high. If you are down low in the street, you escape its fury; but climb to the top of the Monument, or St. Paul's, and try whether you do not feel it. Get into the valley, it is all right. The lower branches of the trees are scarcely moved, but the top branches are rocked to and fro by it. It is a great leveler; so is the Holy Spirit. He never sees a man high but he brings him down. He makes every high thought bow before the majesty of his might; and if you have any high thought tonight, rest assured that when the Spirit of God comes, he will lay it low, even with the ground.

Now, do not let this make you fear the Holy Spirit. It is a blessed thing to be rocked so as to have our hopes tested, and it is a precious thing to have our carnal confidences shaken. And how blessedly the wind *purifies* the atmosphere! In the Swiss valleys there is a heaviness in the air which makes the inhabitants unhealthy. They take quinine, and you see them going about with big swellings in their necks. From Martigny to Bretagne [Switzerland], there is a great valley in which you will see hundreds of persons diseased. The reason is, that the air does not circulate. They are breathing the same air, or some of it, that their fathers breathed before them. There seems to be no ventilation between the two parts of the giant Alps, and the air never circulates; but if they have a great storm which sweeps through the valleys, it is a great blessing to the people. And so the Spirit of God comes and cleanses out our evil thoughts and vain imaginations, and though we do not like the hurricane, yet it brings spiritual health to our soul.

Again the wind is a great *trier of the nature of things*. Here comes a great rushing up the street: it sweeps over the heaps of rubbish lying in the road—away goes all the light chaff, paper, and other things which have no weight in them; they cannot stand the brunt of its whirling power; but see, the pieces of iron, the stones, and all weighty things are left unmoved. In the country you will often see the farmer severing the chaff from the wheat by throwing it up into a current of air, and the light husks all blow away, while the heavy wheat sinks on the heap, cleansed and purified.

So is the Holy Ghost the great testing power, and the result of his operations will be to show men what they are. Here is a hypocrite: he has passed muster hitherto, and reckons himself to be a true and genuine man, but there comes a blast from Heaven's mighty spirit, and he finds himself to be lighter than vanity: he has no weight in him, he is driven on and has no rest, can find no peace, he hurries from one refuge of lies to another. "There is no peace," saith my God, to the wicked. Thus also we try the doctrines of men, we bring the breath of inspiration to bear upon them: do they abide the test, or are they driven away? Can you hold that truth in the presence of God? Can you cling to it and find it stable in the hour of trial? Is it a nice pleasant speculation for a sunny day when all is calm and bright, or will it bear the rough rude blast of adversity, when God's Holy Spirit is purifying you with his healthful influence? True Christians and sound doctrines have ballast and weight in them: they are not moved nor driven away, but empty professors [of faith] and hollow dogmas are scattered like chaff before the wind when the Lord shall blow upon them with the breath of his Spirit. Examine yourselves therefore, try the doctrines and see if they be of God. "What is the chaff to the wheat?" saith the Lord. Have root in yourselves, then will you not wither in the hot blast, nor be driven away in the tempestuous day.

Is not the Spirit moreover like unto the wind in its *developing of character?* See the dust is lying all over the picture, you cannot see the fair features of the beauteous sketch beneath; blow off the dust, and the fine colors will be seen, and once more the skill of the painter will be admired. Have you never noticed some piece of fine mosaic, or perhaps some well cut engraving on metal, all hidden, and the fine lines filled up with dust? You have blown off the accumulation, and then you could admire the work. So does the Spirit of God. Men get all covered with dust in the hot dusty roadside of life till they are nearly the color of the earth itself; but they come to the hill-top of Calvary, and here they stand till the wind of Heaven has cleansed them from all the dust that has gathered around their garments. Oh, there is nothing like communion with the Spirit of God to counteract the earthly tendencies of a business life. There are some men that get covered with a yellow dust, till they are almost hidden by it; they can talk of nothing else but money. Gold, gold, gold, is getting to occupy nearly every thought. Now, I have no quarrel with money in its right place, but I do not like to see men *live* in it. I always try to drive away that mean and groveling spirit which lives for nothing else but to accumulate money, but I cannot always succeed. Now the Spirit of God will make a man see his folly and put his money into its right position, and place the graces of the Christian character where men can see them and glorify God in them. Never let your business character or professional skill dim and hide your Christianity. If you do, God's Spirit will come to brighten you up, and he will have no mercy on these, but will, in love to your soul, cleanse and give luster to God's work which is wrought in you.

I have also noticed how helpful the wind is to all who choose to avail themselves of it. In Lincolnshire, where the country is flat and below the level of the sea, they are obliged to drain the land by means of windmills, and hundreds of them may be seen pumping up the water so as to relieve the land of the excess of moisture. In many parts of the country, nearly all the wheat and corn is ground by means of the wind. If it was not then for the wind, the inhabitants would be put to great inconvenience. The Spirit of God is thus also a mighty helper to all who will avail themselves of his influences. You are inundated with sin, a flood of iniquity comes in; you can never bale out the torrent, but with the help of God's Spirit it can be done. He will so assist, that you shall see the flood gradually descending and your heart once more purified. You need ever to ask his help; fresh sin, like falling showers, will be poured into you by every passing day, and you will need a continuous power to cast it out; you may have it in God's Spirit; he will with ceaseless energy help you to combat against sin, and make you more than a conqueror. Or, on the other hand, if you need some power to break up and prepare for you your spiritual food, you will find no better help than what God's Spirit can give. In Eastern countries they grind corn by the hand, two sitting at a small stone mill; but it is a poor affair at best; so are our own vain attempts to prepare the bread of Heaven for ourselves. We shall only get a little, and that little, badly ground. Commentators are good in their way, but give me the teaching of the Holy Ghost. He makes the passage clear and gives me to eat of the finest of the wheat. How often we have found our utter inability to understand some part of divine truth; we asked some of God's people and they helped us a little, but after all, we were not satisfied till we took it to the throne of heavenly grace, and implored the teachings of the blessed Spirit; then how sweetly it was opened to us; we could eat of it spiritually. It was no longer husk and shell, hard to be understood; it was as bread to us, and we could eat to the full. Brethren, we must make more use of the wisdom which cometh from above, for the Spirit, like the wind, is open to us all, to employ for our own personal benefit.

I see also here a thought as to the co-operation of man and the Spirit in all Christian work. It has pleased God to make us coworkers with him, fellow laborers, both in the matter of our own salvation, and also in the effort to benefit others. Look for a moment at yon stately bark [ship]: she moves not because of her sails, but she would not reach the desired haven without them. It is the wind which propels her forward; but the wind would not act upon her as it does, unless she had the rigging all fixed, her masts standing, and her sails all bent, so as to catch the passing breeze. But now that human seamanship has done its best, see how she flies! She will soon reach her haven with such a favoring gale as that. You have only to stand still and see how the wind bears her on like a thing of life.

And so it is with the human heart. When the Spirit comes to the soul that is ready to receive such influences, then he helps you on to Christian grace and Christian work, and makes you bear up through all opposition, till you come to the port of peace, and can anchor safely there. Without him we can do nothing: without us, He will not work. We are to preach the gospel to every creature, and while one plants, and another waters, God adds the increase. We are to work out our own salvation, but he worketh in us to will and to do of his own good pleasure. We must go up to possess the goodly land with our own spear and sword; but the hornet goes before us to drive out the foe. Jericho shall be captured by a divine and miraculous interference, but even there, rams' horns shall find a work to do, and must be employed. The host of Midian shall be slain, but our cry is, "The sword of the Lord and of Gideon." We give God all the glory: nevertheless we use the means. The water of Jordan must be sought out, and used by all who desire a cleansing like Naaman the Syrian. A lump of figs must be used if other Hezekiahs are to be healed; but the Spirit is, after all, the great Cleanser and Healer of his people Israel. The lesson is clear to all: the wind turns mills that men make; fills sails that human hands have spread; and the Spirit blesses human effort, crowns with success our labors, establishes the work of our hands upon us, and teaches all through, that "the hand of the diligent maketh rich;" but "if a man will not work, neither shall he eat."

Another thought suggests itself to my mind in connection with the wind and human effort; it is this: how completely dependent men are upon the wind as to what it shall do for them. They are entirely at its mercy as to its time of blowing, its strength, and the direction it will take. I have already dwelt upon this thought of the sovereignty of the wind, but it comes up here in a more practical form. The steamer now can steer almost anywhere they please, and at all times it will proceed on its voyage; but the sailing-ship must tack according to the wind, and when becalmed must wait for the breeze to spring up. The water-mill and steam-mill can be worked night and day, but the mill that depends upon the wind must abide by the wind's times of blowing, and must turn round its sails so as to suit the direction of the current of air. In like manner we are compelled to wait the pleasure of the Spirit. There is no reservoir of water which we can turn on when we will, and work as we please. We should forget God far more than we do now if that were the case. The sailor who is depending on the wind anxiously looks up to the masthead to see how the breeze is shifting and turning round the vane; and he scans the heavens to see what weather he is likely to have. He would not need to care nearly so much as he does now that he is absolutely dependent on the wind, if he had steam-power, so as to sail in the very teeth of the storm if he so willed. God, then, keeps us looking up to Heaven by making us to be completely at his mercy as to the times and ways of giving us his helping-power. It is a blessed thing to wait on God, watching for his hand and in quiet contentment, leaving all to him. Brethren, let us do our part faithfully, spread every sail, make all as perfect as human skill and wisdom can direct, and then in patient continuance in well-doing, wait the Spirit's propitious gales, neither murmuring because he tarries, nor be taken unawares when he comes upon us in his sovereign pleasure to do that which seemeth good in his sight.

Now, tonight I have only given you some hints on this subject: you can work it out for yourselves. As you hear the wind, you may get more sermons out of it than I can give you just now. The thing is perfectly inexhaustible; and I think the business of the minister is not to say all that can be said about the subject. Somebody remarked concerning a certain minister, that he was a most unfair preacher, because he always exhausted the subject and left nothing for anybody else to say. That will never be said of me, and I would rather that it should not. A minister should suggest germs of thought, open up new ways, and present, if possible, the truth in such a method as to lead men to understand that the half is not told them.

And now, my dear hearer, whether you listen often to my voice, or have now stepped in for the first time, I would like to ring this in your ear, Dost thou know the Spirit of God? If ye have not the Spirit, ye are none of his. "Ye must be born again." "What, Lord—'must?' Dost thou not mean 'may?'" No, ye *must*. "Does it not mean, 'Ye can be?'" No, ye *must*. When a man says, "must," it all depends upon who he is. When God says, *"must,"* there it stands, and it cannot be questioned. There are the flames of Hell: would you escape from them? You must be born again. There are Heaven's glories sparkling in their own light: would you enjoy them? You must be born again. There is the peace and joy of a believer: would you have it? You must be born again. What, not a crumb from off the table without this? No, not one. Not a drop of water to cool your burning tongues except you are born again. This is the one condition that never moves. God never alters it, and never will. You must, *must*, MUST. Which shall it be? Shall your will stand, or God's will? O, let God's "must" ride right over you, and bow yourselves down, and say,

Lord, I must, then I will; ah! and it has come to this—I must tonight. Give me Christ, or else I die. I have hold of the knocker of the door of thy mercy, and I must, I *will* get that door open. I will never let thee go except thou bless me. Thou sayest *must*, Lord, and I say *must* too.

"Ye must, ye must be born again." God fulfill the "must" in each of your cases, for Jesus Christ's sake. Amen.

The Withering Work of the Spirit

Delivered on Lord's Day morning, July 9, 1871, at the Metropolitan Tabernacle, Newington. No. 999.

The voice said, "Cry." And he said, "What shall I cry?" "All flesh is grass, and all the goodliness thereof is as the flower of the field: the grass withereth, the flower fadeth: because the Spirit of the Lord bloweth upon it: surely the people is grass. The grass withereth, the flower fadeth: but the word of our God shall stand forever."—Isaiah 40:6–8

Being born again, not of corruptible seed, but of incorruptible, by the word of God, which liveth and abideth forever. For all flesh is as grass, and all the glory of man as the flower of grass. The grass withereth, and the flower thereof falleth away: but the word of the Lord endureth forever. And this is the word which by the gospel is preached unto you.—1 Peter 1:23–25

The passage in Isaiah which I have just read in your hearing may be used as a very eloquent description of our mortality, and if a sermon should be preached from it upon the frailty of human nature, the brevity of life, and the certainty of death, no one could dispute the appropriateness of the text. Yet I venture to question whether such a discourse would strike the central teaching of the prophet. Something more than the decay of our material flesh is intended here; the carnal mind, the flesh in another sense, was intended by the Holy Ghost when he bade his messenger proclaim those words. It does not seem to me that a mere expression of the mortality of our race was needed in this place, by the context; it would hardly keep pace with the sublime revelations which surround it, and would in some measure be a digression from the subject in hand. The notion that we are here [in this passage] simply and alone reminded of our mortality does not square with the New Testament exposition of it in Peter, which I have also placed before you as a text. There is another and more spiritual meaning here beside and beyond that which would be contained in the great and very obvious truth that all of us must die.

Look at the chapter in Isaiah with care. What is the subject of it? It is the divine consolation of Zion. Zion had been tossed to and fro with conflicts; she had been smarting under the result of sin. The Lord, to remove her sorrow, bids his prophets announce the coming of the long-expected Deliverer, the end and accomplishment of all her warfare, and the pardon of all her iniquity. There is no doubt that this is the theme of the prophecy; and further, there is no sort of question about the next point, that the prophet goes on to foretell the coming of John the Baptist as the harbinger of the Messiah. We have no difficulty in the explanation of the passage, "Prepare ye the way of the Lord, make straight in the desert a highway for our God;" for the New Testament again and again refers this to the Baptist and his ministry. The object of the coming of the Baptist and the mission of the Messiah, whom he heralded, was the manifestation of divine glory. Observe the fifth verse: "The glory of the Lord shall be revealed, and all flesh shall see it together: for the mouth of the Lord hath spoken it." Well, what next? Was it needful to mention man's mortality in this connection? We think not. But there is much more appropriateness in the succeeding verses, if we see their deeper meaning. Do they not mean this? *In order to make room for the display of the divine glory in Christ Jesus and his salvation, there would come a withering of all the glory wherein man boasts himself: the flesh should be seen in its true nature as corrupt and dying, and the grace of God alone should be exalted.* This would be seen under the ministry of John the Baptist first, and should be the preparatory work of the Holy Ghost in men's hearts, in all time, in order that the glory of the Lord should be revealed and human pride be forever confounded.

The Spirit blows upon the flesh, and that which seemed vigorous becomes weak, that which was fair to look upon is smitten with decay; the true nature of the flesh is thus discovered, its deceit is laid bare, its power is destroyed, and there is space for the dispensation of the ever-abiding word, and for the rule of the Great Shepherd, whose words are spirit and life.

There is a withering wrought by the Spirit which is the preparation for the sowing and implanting by which salvation is wrought.

The withering before the sowing was very marvelously fulfilled in the preaching of John the Baptist. Most appropriately he carried on his ministry in the desert, for a spiritual desert was all around him; he was the voice of one crying in the wilderness. It was not his work to plant, but to hew down. The fleshly religion of the Jews was then in its prime. Phariseeism stalked through the streets in all its pomp; men complacently rested in outward ceremonies only, and spiritual religion was at the lowest conceivable ebb. Here and there might be found a Simeon and an Anna, but for the most part men knew nothing of spiritual religion, but said in their hearts: "We have Abraham to our father," and this is enough. What a stir he [Jesus] made when he called the lordly Pharisees a generation of vipers! How he shook the nation with the declaration, "Now also the axe is laid unto the root of the trees"! Stern as Elias [Elijah], his work was to level the mountains, and lay low every lofty imagination. That word, "Repent," was as a scorching wind to the verdure of self-righteousness, a killing blast for the confidence of ceremonialism. His food and his dress called for fasting and mourning. The outward token of his ministry declared the death amid which he preached, as he buried in the waters of Jordan those who came to him. "Ye must die and be buried, even as he who is to come will save by death and burial." This was the meaning of the emblem which he set before the crowd. His typical act was as thorough in its teaching as were his words; and as if that were not enough, he warned them of a yet more searching and trying baptism with the Holy Ghost and with fire, and of the coming of one whose fan was in his hand, thoroughly to purge his floor. The Spirit in John blew as the rough north wind, searching and withering, and made him to be a destroyer of the vain gloryings of a fleshly religion, that the spiritual faith might be established.

When our Lord himself actually appeared, he came into a withered land, whose glories had all departed. Old Jesse's stem was bare, and our Lord was the branch which grew out of his root. The scepter had departed from Judah, and the lawgiver from between his feet, when Shiloh came. An alien sat on David's throne, and the Roman called the covenant-land his own. The lamp of prophecy burned but dimly, even if it had not utterly gone out. No Isaiah had arisen of late to console them, nor even a Jeremiah to lament their apostasy. The whole economy of Judaism was as a worn-out vesture; it had waxed old, and was ready to vanish away. The priesthood was disarranged. Luke tells us that Annas and Caiaphas were high priests that year—two in a year or at once, a strange setting aside of the laws of Moses. All the dispensation which gathered around the visible, or, as Paul calls it, the "worldly" sanctuary, was coming to a close; and when our Lord had finished his work, the veil of the temple was rent in twain, the sacrifices were abolished, the priesthood of Aaron was set aside, and carnal ordinances were abrogated, for the Spirit revealed spiritual things. When he came, who was made a priest, "not after the law of a carnal commandment, but after the power of an endless life," there was "a disannulling of the commandment going before for the weakness and unprofitableness thereof."

Such are the facts of history; but I am not about to dilate upon them: I am coming to your own personal histories—to the experience of every child of God. In every one of us it must be fulfilled, that all that is of the flesh in us, seeing it is but as grass, must be withered, and the comeliness thereof must be destroyed. The Spirit of God, like the wind, must pass over the field of our souls, and cause our beauty to be as a fading flower. He must so convince us of sin, and so reveal ourselves to ourselves, that we shall see that the flesh profiteth nothing; that our fallen nature is corruption itself, and that "they who are in the flesh cannot please God." There must be brought home to us the sentence of death upon our former legal and carnal life, that the incorruptible seed of the word of God, implanted by the Holy Ghost, may be in us, and abide in us forever.

The subject of this morning is the withering work of the Spirit upon the souls of men, and when we have spoken upon it, we shall conclude with a few words upon the implanting work, which always follows where this withering work has been performed.

I. Turning then to *the work of the Spirit in causing the goodliness of the flesh to fade,* let us, first, observe that the work of the Holy Spirit upon the soul of man in withering up that which is of the flesh, is *very unexpected.*

1. You will observe in our text that even the speaker himself, though doubtless one taught of God, when he was bidden to cry, said, *"What shall I cry?"* Even he did not know that, in order to the comforting of God's people, there must first be experienced a preliminary visitation. Many preachers of God's gospel have forgotten that the law is the schoolmaster to bring men to Christ. They have sown on the unbroken fallow ground and forgotten that the plough must break the clods. We have seen too much of trying to sew without the sharp needle of the Spirit's convincing power. Preachers have labored to make Christ precious to those who think themselves rich and increased in goods: and it has been labor in vain. It is our duty to preach Jesus Christ even to self-righteous sinners, but it is certain that Jesus Christ will never be accepted by them while they hold themselves in high esteem. Only the sick will welcome the physician. It is the work of the Spirit of God to convince men of sin, and until they are convinced of sin, they will never be led to seek the righteousness which is of God by Jesus Christ. I am persuaded, that wherever there is a real work of grace in any soul, it begins with a pulling down: the Holy Ghost does not build on the old foundation. Wood, hay, and stubble will not do for him to build upon. He will come as the fire, and cause a conflagration of all proud nature's Babels. He will break our bow and cut our spear in sunder, and burn our chariot in the fire. When every sandy foundation is gone, then, but not till then,

behold he will lay in our souls the great foundation stone, chosen of God, and precious. The awakened sinner, when he asks that God would have mercy upon him, is much astonished to find that, instead of enjoying a speedy peace, his soul is bowed down within him under a sense of divine wrath. Naturally enough he enquires:

> Is this the answer to my prayer? I prayed the Lord to deliver me from sin and self, and is this the way in which he deals with me? I said, "Hear me," and behold he wounds me with the wounds of a cruel one. I said, "Clothe me," and lo! He has torn off from me the few rags which covered me before, and my nakedness stares me in the face. I said, "Wash me," and behold he has plunged me in the ditch till mine own clothes do abhor me. Is this the way of grace?

Sinner, be not surprised: it is even so. Perceivest thou not the cause of it? How canst thou be healed while the proud flesh is in thy wound? It must come out. It is the only way to heal thee permanently: it would be folly to film over thy sore, or heal thy flesh, and leave the leprosy within thy bones. The great physician will cut with his sharp knife till the corrupt flesh be removed, for only thus can a sure healing work be wrought in thee. Dost thou not see that it is divinely wise that before thou art clothed, thou shouldst be stripped! What, wouldst thou have Christ's lustrous righteousness outside whiter than any fuller can make it, and thine own filthy rags concealed within? Nay, man; they must be put away; not a single thread of thine own must be left upon thee. It cannot be that God should cleanse thee until he has made thee see somewhat of thy defilement; for thou wouldst never value the precious blood which cleanses us from all sin if thou hadst not first of all been made to mourn that thou art altogether an unclean thing.

The convincing work of the Spirit, wherever it comes, is unexpected, and even to the child of God in whom this process has still to go on, it is often startling. We begin again to build that which the Spirit of God had destroyed. Having begun in the spirit, we act as if we would be made perfect in the flesh; and then when our mistaken upbuilding has to be leveled with the earth, we are almost as astonished as we were when first the scales fell from our eyes. In some such condition as this was Newton when he wrote:—

> *I asked the Lord that I might grow*
> *In faith and love and every grace,*
> *Might more of his salvation know,*
> *And seek more earnestly his face.*
>
> *Twas he who taught me thus to pray,*
> *And he, I trust, has answered prayer;*
> *But it has been in such a way*
> *As almost drove me to despair.*

> *I hop'd that in some favor'd hour,*
> *At once he'd answer my request,*
> *And by his love's constraining power*
> *Subdue my sins, and give me rest.*
>
> *Instead of this, he made me feel*
> *The hidden evils of my heart,*
> *And let the angry powers of hell*
> *Assault my soul in ev'ry part.*

Ah, marvel not, for thus the Lord is wont to answer his people. The voice which saith, "Comfort ye, comfort ye my people," achieves its purpose by first making them hear the cry, "All flesh is grass, and all the goodliness thereof is as the flower of the field."

2. Furthermore, this withering is *after the usual order of the divine operation*. If we consider well the way of God, we shall not be astonished that he beginneth with his people by terrible things in righteousness. Observe the method of creation. I will not venture upon any dogmatic theory of geology, but there seems to be every probability that this world has been fitted up and destroyed, refitted and then destroyed again, many times before the last arranging of it for the habitation of men. "In the beginning God created the Heaven and the earth;" then came a long interval, and at length, at the appointed time, during seven days, the Lord prepared the earth for the human race. Consider then the state of matters when the great architect began his work. What was there in the beginning? Originally, nothing. When he commanded the ordering of the earth how was it? "The earth was without form and void; and darkness was upon the face of the deep." There was no trace of another's plan to interfere with the great architect.

> With whom took he counsel, and who instructed him, and taught him in the path of judgment, and taught him knowledge, and showed to him the way of understanding?

He received no contribution of column or pillar towards the temple which he intended to build. The earth was, as the Hebrew puts it, *Tohu* and *Bohu*, disorder and confusion—in a word, chaos. So it is in the new creation. When the Lord new creates us, he borrows nothing from the old man, but makes all things new. He does not repair and add a new wing to the old house of our depraved nature, but he builds a new temple for his own praise. We are spiritually without form and empty, and darkness is upon the face of our heart, and his word comes to us, saying, "Light be," and there is light, and ere long, life and every precious thing.

To take another instance from the ways of God. When man has fallen, when did the Lord bring him the gospel? The first whisper of the gospel, as you know, was, "I will put enmity between thee and the woman, between thy seed and her seed. He shall bruise thy head." That whisper came to man shivering in the presence of his Maker, having nothing more to say by way of excuse; but standing guilty before the Lord. When did the Lord God clothe our parents? Not until first of all he had put the question, "Who told thee that thou wast naked?" Not until the fig-leaves had utterly failed did the Lord bring in the covering skin of the sacrifice, and wrap them in it. If you will pursue the meditation upon the acts of God with men, you will constantly see the same thing. God has given us a wonderful type of salvation in Noah's ark; but Noah was saved in that ark in connection with death; he himself, as it were, immured alive in a tomb, and all the world besides left to destruction. All other hope for Noah was gone, and then the ark rose upon the waters. Remember the redemption of the children of Israel out of Egypt: it occurred when they were in the saddest plight, and their cry went up to Heaven by reason of their bondage. When no arm brought salvation, then with a high hand and an outstretched arm, the Lord brought forth his people. Everywhere, before the salvation there comes the humbling of the creature, the overthrow of human hope. As in the backwoods of America, before there can be tillage, the planting of cities, the arts of civilization, and the transactions of commerce—the woodman's axe must hack and hew: the stately trees of centuries must fall: the roots must be burned, the odd reign of nature disturbed. The old must go before the new can come. Even thus the Lord takes away the first, that he may establish the second. The first Heaven and the first Earth must pass away, or there cannot be a new Heaven and a new Earth. Now, as it has been outwardly, we ought to expect that it would be the same within us, and when these witherings and fadings occur in our souls, we should only say "It is the Lord, let him do as seemeth him good."

3. *I would have you notice, thirdly, that we are taught in our text* how universal this process is in its range *over the hearts of all those upon whom the Spirit works*. The withering is a withering of what? Of *part* of the flesh and some portion of its tendencies? Nay, observe, "*All* flesh is grass; and *all* the goodliness thereof"—the very choice and pick of it—"is as the flower of the field," and what happens to the grass? Does any of it live? "The grass withereth," all of it. The flower, will not that abide? So fair a thing, has not that an immortality? No, it fades: it utterly falls away. So wherever the Spirit of God breathes on the soul of man, there is a withering of everything that is of the flesh, and it is seen that, to be carnally minded, is death. Of course, we all know and confess that where there is a work of grace, there must be a destruction of our delight in the pleasures of the flesh. When the Spirit of God breathes on us, that which was sweet becomes bitter; that which was bright becomes dim. A man cannot love sin and yet possess the life of God. If he takes pleasure in fleshly joys wherein he once delighted, he is still what he was: he minds the things of the flesh, and therefore he is after the flesh, and he shall die. The world and the lusts thereof are to the unregenerate as beautiful as the meadows in spring, when they are bedecked with flowers, but to the regenerate soul they are a wilderness, a salt land, and not inhabited. Of those very things wherein we once took delight we say,

"Vanity of vanities; all is vanity." We cry to be delivered from the poisonous joys of earth, we loathe them, and wonder that we could once riot in them. Beloved hearers, do you know what this kind of withering means? Have you seen the lusts of the flesh, and the pomps and the pleasures thereof all fade away before your eyes? It must be so, or the Spirit of God has not visited your soul.

But mark, wherever the Spirit of God comes, he destroys the goodliness and flower of the flesh; that is to say, our righteousness withers as our sinfulness. Before the Spirit comes, we think ourselves as good as the best. We say, "All these commandments have I kept from my youth up," and we superciliously ask, "What lack I yet?" Have we not been moral? Nay, have we not even been religious? We confess that we may have committed faults, but we think them very venial, and we venture, in our wicked pride, to imagine that, after all, we are not so vile as the word of God would lead us to think. Ah, my dear hearer, when the Spirit of God blows on the comeliness of thy flesh, its beauty will fade as a leaf, and thou wilt have quite another idea of thyself—thou wilt then find no language too severe in which to describe thy past character. Searching deep into thy motives, and investigating that which moved thee to thine actions, thou wilt see so much of evil, that thou wilt cry with the publican, "God be merciful to me, a sinner!"

Where the Holy Ghost has withered up in us our self-righteousness, he has not half completed his work; there is much more to be destroyed yet, and among the rest, away must go our boasted power of resolution. Most people conceive that they can turn to God whenever they resolve to do so. "I am a man of such strength of mind," says one, "that if I made up my mind to be religious, I should be without difficulty." "Ah," saith another volatile spirit, "I believe that one of these days I can correct the errors of the past, and commence a new life." Ah, dear hearers, the resolutions of the flesh are goodly flowers, but they must all fade. When visited by the Spirit of God, we find that even when the will is present with us, how to perform that which we would, we find not; yea, and we discover that our will is averse to all that is good, and that naturally we will not come unto Christ that we may have life. What poor frail things resolutions are when seen in the light of God's Spirit!

Still the man will say,

> I believe I have, after all, within myself an enlightened conscience and an intelligence that will guide me aright. The light of nature I will use, and I do not doubt that if I wander somewhat I shall find my way back again.

Ah, man! thy wisdom, which is the very flower of thy nature, what is it but folly, though thou knowest it not? Unconverted and unrenewed, thou art in God's sight no wiser than the wild ass's colt. I wish thou wert in thine own esteem humbled as a little child at Jesus' feet, and made to cry, "Teach thou me."

When the withering wind of the Spirit moves over the carnal mind, it reveals the death of the flesh in all respects, especially in the matter of power towards that which is good. We then learn that word of our Lord: "Without me ye can do nothing." When I was seeking the Lord, I not only *believed* that I could not pray without divine help, but I *felt* in my very soul that I could not. Then I could not even feel aright, or mourn as I would, or groan as I would. I longed to long more after Christ; but, alas! I could not even feel that I needed him as I ought to feel it. This heart was then as har,d as adamant, as dead, as those that rot in their graves. Oh, what would I at times have given for a tear! I wanted to repent, but could not; longed to believe, but could not; I felt bound, hampered, and paralyzed. This is a humbling revelation of God's Holy Spirit, but a needful one; for the faith of the flesh is not the faith of God's elect. The faith which justifies the soul is the gift of God and not of ourselves. That repentance which is the work of the flesh will need to be repented of. The flower of the flesh must wither; only the seed of the Spirit will produce fruit unto perfection. The heirs of Heaven are born not of blood, nor of the will of the flesh, nor of man, but of God. If the work in us be not the Spirit's working, but our own, it will droop and die when most we require its protection; and its end will be as the grass, which today is, and tomorrow is cast into the oven.

4. *You see, then, the universality of this withering work within us, but I beg you also to notice the completeness of it.* The grass, what does it do? Droop? Nay, wither. The flower of the field: what of that? Does it hang its head a little? No, according to Isaiah it fades; and according to Peter it falleth away. There is no reviving it with showers, it has come to its end. Even thus are the awakened led to see that in their flesh there dwelleth no good thing. What dying and withering work some of God's servants have had in their souls! Look at John Bunyan, as he describes himself in his *Grace Abounding!* For how many months and even years was the Spirit engaged in writing death upon all that was the old Bunyan, in order that he might become by grace a new man fitted to track the pilgrims along their heavenly way. We have not all endured the ordeal so long, but in every child of God there must be a death to sin, to the law, and to self, which must be fully accomplished ere he is perfected in Christ and taken to Heaven. Corruption cannot inherit incorruption; it is through the Spirit that we mortify the deeds of the body, and therefore live. But cannot the fleshly mind be improved? By no means; for "the carnal mind is enmity against God: for it is not subject to the law of God, neither indeed can be." Cannot you improve the old nature? No; "ye must be born again." Can it not be taught heavenly things? No. "The natural man receiveth not the things of the Spirit of God: for they are foolishness unto him: neither can he know them, because they are spiritually discerned." There is nothing to be done with the old nature but to let it be laid in the grave; it must be dead, and buried, and when it is so, then the incorruptible seed that liveth and abideth forever will develop gloriously, the fruit of the new birth will come to maturity, and grace shall be exalted in glory. The old nature never does improve: it is as earthly, and sensual, and devilish in the saint of eighty

years of age as it was when first he came to Christ; it is unimproved and unimprovable; towards God it is enmity itself: every imagination of the thoughts of the heart is evil, and that continually. The old nature called "the flesh lusteth against the Spirit, and the Spirit against the flesh: and these are contrary the one to the other," neither can there be peace between them.

5. Let us further notice that all this withering work in the soul is very painful. As you read these verses, do they not strike you as having a very funereal tone? "All flesh is grass, and all the goodliness thereof is as the flower of the field: the grass withereth, the flower fadeth." This is mournful work, but it must be done. I think those who experience much of it when they first come to Christ have great reason to be thankful. Their course in life will, in all probability, be much brighter and happier, for I have noticed that persons who are converted very easily, and come to Christ with but comparatively little knowledge of their own depravity, have to learn it afterwards, and they remain for a long time babes in Christ, and are perplexed with matters that would not have troubled them if they had experienced a deeper work at first. No, sir; if grace has begun to build in your soul and left any of the old walls of self-trust standing, they will have to come down sooner or later. You may congratulate yourself upon their remaining, but it is a false congratulation, your glorying is not good. I am sure of this, that Christ will never put a new piece upon an old garment, or new wine in old bottles: he knows the rent would be worse in the long run, and the bottles would burst. All that is of nature's spinning must be unraveled. The natural building must come down, lath and plaster, roof and foundation, and we must have a house not made with hands. It was a great mercy for our city of London that the great fire cleared away all the old buildings which were the lair of the plague—a far healthier city was then built; and it is a great mercy for a man when God sweeps right away all his own righteousness and strength, when he makes him feel that he is nothing and can be nothing, and drives him to confess that Christ must be all in all, and that his only strength lies in the eternal might of the ever-blessed Spirit.

Sometimes in a house of business, an old system has been going on for years, and it has caused much confusion, and allowed much dishonesty. You come in as a new manager, and you adopt an entirely new plan. Now, try if you can, and graft your method on to the old system. How it will worry you! Year after year you say to yourself, "I cannot work it: if I had swept the whole away and started afresh, clear from the beginning, it would not have given me one-tenth of the trouble." God does not intend to graft the system of grace upon corrupt nature, nor to make the new Adam grow out of the old Adam, but he intends to teach us this: "Ye are dead, and your life is hid with Christ in God." Salvation is not of the flesh but of the Lord alone; that which is born of the flesh is only flesh at the best; and only that which is born of the Spirit is spirit. It must be the Spirit's work altogether, or it is not what God will accept.

6. *Observe, brethren, that although this is painful,* it is inevitable. I have already entrenched upon this, and shown you how necessary it is that all of the old should be taken away; but let me further remark that it is inevitable that the old should go, because it is in itself corruptible. Why does the grass wither? Because it is a withering thing. "Its root is ever in its grave, and it must die." How could it spring out of the earth, and be immortal? It is no amaranth:[1] it blooms not in Paradise: it grows in a soil on which the curse has fallen. Every supposed good thing that grows out of your own self is, like yourself, mortal—and it must die. The seeds of corruption are in all the fruits of manhood's tree; let them be as fair to look upon as Eden's clusters, they must decay.

Moreover, it would never do, my brother, that there should be something of the flesh in our salvation and something of the Spirit; for if it were so, there would be a division of the honor. Hitherto the praises of God; beyond this, my own praises. If I were to win Heaven partly through what I had done, and partly through what Christ had done, and if the energy which sanctified me was in a measure my own, and in a measure divine, they that divide the work shall divide the reward, and the songs of Heaven while they would be partly to Jehovah must also be partly to the creature. But it shall not be. "Down, proud flesh! Down!" I say.

> Though thou cleanse and purge thyself as thou mayst, thou art to the core corrupt; though thou labor unto weariness, thou buildest wood that will be burned, and stubble that will be turned to ashes. Give up thine own self-confidence, and let the work be, and the merit be where the honor shall be, namely, with God alone.

It is inevitable, then, that there should be all this withering.

7. This last word is *by way of comfort* to any that are passing through the process we are describing, and I hope some of you are. It gives me great joy when I hear that you unconverted ones are very miserable, for the miseries which the Holy Spirit works are always the prelude to happiness. *It is the Spirit's work to wither.* I rejoice in our translation, "Because the Spirit of the Lord bloweth upon it." It is true the passage may be translated, "The wind of the Lord bloweth upon it." One word, as you know, is used in the Hebrew both for "wind" and "Spirit," and the same is true of the Greek; but let us retain the old translation here, for I conceive it to be the real meaning of the text. The Spirit of God it is that withers the flesh. It is not the devil that killed my self-righteousness. I might be afraid if it were: nor was it myself that humbled myself by a voluntary and needless self-degradation, but it was the Spirit of God. Better to be broken in pieces by the Spirit of God, than to be made whole by the flesh! What doth the Lord say? "I kill." But what next? "I make

---
[1] Amaranth: imaginary flower that never fades.

alive." He never makes any alive but those he kills. Blessed be the Holy Ghost when he kills me, when he drives the sword through the very bowels of my own merits and my self-confidence, for then he will make me alive. "I wound, and I heal." He never heals those whom he has not wounded. Then blessed be the hand that wounds; let it go on wounding; let it cut and tear; let it lay bare to me myself at my very worst, that I may be driven to self-despair, and may fall back upon the free mercy of God, and receive it as a poor, guilty, lost, helpless, undone sinner, who casts himself into the arms of sovereign grace, knowing that God must give all, and Christ must be all, and the Spirit must work all, and man must be as clay in the potter's hands, that the Lord may do with him as seemeth to him good. Rejoice, dear brother, how ever low you are brought, for if the Spirit humbles you, he means no evil, but he intends infinite good to your soul.

II. Now, let us close with a few sentences concerning *the implantation*.

According to Peter, although the flesh withers, and the flower thereof falls away, yet in the children of God there is an *un*withering something of another kind. "Being born again, not of corruptible seed, but of incorruptible, by the word of God, which liveth and abideth forever." "The word of the Lord endureth forever. And this is the word which by the gospel is preached unto you." Now, the gospel is of use to us because it is not of human origin. If it were of the flesh, all it could do for us would not land us beyond the flesh; but the gospel of Jesus Christ is super-human, divine, and spiritual. In its conception it was of God; its great gift, even the Savior, is a divine gift; and all its teachings are full of deity. If you, my hearer, believe a gospel which you have thought out for yourself, or a philosophical gospel which comes from the brain of man, it is of the flesh, and will wither, and you will die, and be lost through trusting in it. The only word that can bless you and be a seed in your soul must be the living and incorruptible word of the eternal Spirit. Now this is the incorruptible word, that "God was made flesh and dwelt among us;" that "God was in Christ, reconciling the world unto himself, not imputing their trespasses unto them." This is the incorruptible word, that "Whosoever believeth that Jesus is the Christ, is born of God." "He that believeth on him is not condemned: but he that believeth not is condemned already, because he hath not believed in the name of the only begotten Son of God." "God hath given to us eternal life, and this life is in his Son." Now, brethren, this is the seed; but before it can grow in your soul, it must be planted there by the Spirit. Do you receive it this morning? Then the Holy Spirit implants it in your soul. Do you leap up to it, and say, "I believe it! I grasp it! On the incarnate God I fix my hope; the substitutionary sacrifice, the complete atonement of Christ is all my confidence; I am reconciled to God by the blood of Jesus." Then you possess the living seed within your soul.

And what is the result of it? Why, then there comes, according to the text, a new life into us, as the result of the indwelling of the living word, and our being born again by it. A new life it is; it is not the old nature putting out its better parts; not the old Adam refining and purifying itself, and rising to something better. No; have we not said aforetime that the flesh withers and the flower thereof fades? It is an entirely new life. Ye are as much new creatures, at your regeneration, as if you had never existed, and had been for the first time created. "Old things are passed away; behold, all things are become new." The child of God is beyond and above other men. Other men do not possess the life which he has received. They are but duplex—body and soul have they. He is of triple nature—he is spirit, soul, and body. A fresh principle, a spark of the divine life has dropped into his soul; he is no longer a natural or carnal man, but he has become a spiritual man, understanding spiritual things and possessing a life far superior to anything that belongs to the rest of mankind. O that God, who has withered in the souls of any of you that which is of the flesh, may speedily grant you the new birth through the Word.

Now observe, to close, wherever this new life comes through the word, it is incorruptible, it lives and abides forever. To get the good seed out of a true believer's heart and to destroy the new nature in him, is a thing attempted by earth and hell, but never yet achieved. Pluck the sun out of the firmament, and you shall not even then be able to pluck grace out of a regenerate heart. It "liveth and abideth forever," saith the text; it neither can corrupt of itself nor be corrupted. "It sinneth not, because it is born of God." "I give unto them eternal life, and they shall never perish, neither shall any man pluck them out of my hand." "The water that I shall give him shall be in him a well of water springing up into everlasting life." You have a natural life—that will die, it is of the flesh. You have a spiritual life—of that it is written: "'Whosoever liveth and believeth in me shall never die." You have now within you the noblest and truest immortality: you must live as God liveth, in peace and joy, and happiness. But oh, remember, dear hearer, if you have not this, you "shall not see life." What then—shall you be annihilated? Ah! no, but "the wrath of the Lord is upon you." You shall exist, though you shall not live. Of life you shall know nothing, for that is the gift of God in Christ Jesus; but of an everlasting death, full of torment and anguish, you shall be the wretched heritor—"the wrath of God abideth on him." You shall be cast into "the lake of fire, which is the second death." You shall be one of those whose "worm dieth not, and whose fire is not quenched." May God, the ever-blessed Spirit, visit you! If he be now striving with you, O quench not his divine flame! Trifle not with any holy thought you have. If this morning you must confess that you are not born again, be humbled by it. Go and seek mercy of the Lord, entreat him to deal graciously with you, and save you. Many who have had nothing but moonlight have prized it, and ere long they have had sunlight. Above all, remember what the quickening seed is, and reverence it when you hear it preached, "for this is the word which by the gospel is preached unto you." Respect it, and receive it. Remember that the quickening seed is all wrapped up in this sentence: "Believe in the Lord Jesus Christ, and thou shalt be saved." "He that believeth and is baptised shall be saved; but he that believeth not shall be damned."

The Lord bless you, for Jesus' sake. Amen.

The Pentecostal Wind and Fire

Delivered on Lord's Day morning, September 18, 1881, at the Metropolitan Tabernacle, Newington. No. 1619.

And suddenly there came a sound from Heaven as of a rushing mighty wind, and it filled all the house where they were sitting. And there appeared unto them cloven tongues like as of fire, and it sat upon each of them. And they were all filled with the Holy Ghost, and began to speak with other tongues, as the Spirit gave them utterance.—Acts 2:2–4

From the descent of the Holy Ghost at the beginning we may learn something concerning his operations at the present time. Remember at the outset that whatever the Holy Spirit was at the first that he is now, for as God he remaineth forever the same: whatsoever he then did he is able to do still, for his power is by no means diminished. As saith the prophet Micah, "O thou that art named the house of Jacob, is the spirit of the Lord straitened?" We should greatly grieve the Holy Spirit if we supposed that his might was less today than in the beginning. Although we may not expect, and need not desire, the miracles which came with the gift of the Holy Spirit, so far as they were physical, yet we may both desire and expect that which was intended and symbolized by them, and we may reckon to see the like spiritual wonders performed among us at this day.

Pentecost, according to the belief of the Jews, was the time of the giving of the law; and if, when the law was given, there was a marvelous display of power on Sinai, it was to be expected that, when the gospel was given—whose ministration is far more glorious—there should be some special unveiling of the divine presence. If at the commencement of the gospel we behold the Holy Spirit working great signs and wonders, may we not expect a continuance—nay, if anything an increased display of his power, as the ages roll on? The law vanished away, but the gospel will never vanish; it shineth more and more to the perfect millennial day; therefore, I reckon that, with the sole exception of physical miracles, whatever was wrought by the Holy Ghost at the first, we may look to be wrought continually while the dispensation lasts. It ought not to be forgotten that Pentecost was the feast of first fruits; it was the time when the first ears of ripe corn were offered unto God. If, then, at the commencement of the gospel harvest we see so plainly the power of the Holy Spirit, may we not most properly expect infinitely more as the harvest advances, and most of all when the most numerous sheaves shall be ingathered? May we not conclude that if the Pentecost was thus marvelous, the actual harvest will be more wonderful still?

This morning my object is not to talk of the descent of the Holy Spirit as a piece of history, but to view it as a fact bearing upon us at this hour, even upon us who are called in these latter days to bear our testimony for the truth. The Father hath sent us the Comforter that he may dwell in us till the coming of the Lord. The Holy Ghost has never *returned,* for he came in accordance with the Savior's prayer, to abide with us forever. The gift of the Comforter was not temporary, and the display of his power was not to be once seen and [then] no more. The Holy Ghost is here, and we ought to expect his divine working among us: and if he does not so work, we should search ourselves to see what it is that hindereth, and whether there may not be somewhat in ourselves which vexes him, so that he restrains his sacred energy, and doth not work among us as he did aforetime. May God grant that the meditation of this morning may increase our faith in the Holy Ghost, and inflame our desires towards him, so that we may look to see him fulfilling his mission among men as at the beginning.

I. First, I shall call your attention to *the instructive symbols* of the Holy Spirit, which were made prominent at Pentecost.

They were two. There was a sound as of a rushing mighty wind, and there were cloven tongues as it were of fire.

Take the symbols separately. The first is *wind*—an emblem of Deity, and therefore a proper symbol of the Holy Spirit. Often under the Old Testament God revealed himself under the emblem of breath or wind: indeed, as most of you know, the Hebrew word for "wind" and "spirit" is the same. So, with the Greek word, when Christ talked to Nicodemus, it is not very easy for translators to tell us when he said "spirit" and when he said "wind;" indeed, some most correctly render the original all the way through by the word "wind," while others with much reason have also used the word "spirit" in their translation. The original word signified either the one or the other, or both. Wind is, of all material things, one of the most spiritual in appearance; it is invisible, ethereal, mysterious; hence, men have fixed upon it as being nearest akin to spirit. In Ezekiel's famous vision, when he saw the valley full of dry bones, we all know that the Spirit of God was intended by that vivifying wind, which came when the prophet prophesied, and blew upon the withered relics till they were quickened into life. "The Lord hath his way in the whirlwind," thus he displays himself when he works. "The Lord answered Job out of the whirlwind," thus he reveals himself when he teaches his servants.

Observe that this wind was, on the day of Pentecost, accompanied with a sound—a sound as of a rushing mighty wind; for albeit the Spirit of God can work in silence, yet in saving operations he frequently uses sound. I would be the last to depreciate meetings in which there is nothing but holy silence, for I could wish that we had more reverence for silence, and it is in stillness that the inner life is nourished; yet the Holy Ghost does not work for the advancement of the kingdom of God by silence alone, for faith cometh by hearing. There is a sound as of a rushing, mighty wind, when the word is sounded forth throughout whole nations by the publishing of the gospel. If the Lord had not given men ears or tongues, silent worship would have been not only appropriate but necessary, but inasmuch as we have ears, the Lord must have intended us to hear something, and as we have tongues, he must have meant us to speak. Some of us would be glad to be quiet, but where the gospel has free course, there is sure to be a measure of noise and stir. The sound came on this occasion, no doubt, to call the attention of the assembly to what was about to occur, to arouse them, and to fill them with awe! There is something indescribably solemn about the rush of a rising tempest; it bows the soul before the sublime mystery of divine power. What more fitting as an attendant upon divine working than the deeply solemn rush of a mighty wind?

With this awe-inspiring sound as of a mighty wind, there was clear indication of its coming from heaven. Ordinary winds blow from this or that quarter of the skies, but this descended from Heaven itself: it was distinctly like a down-draught from above. This sets forth the fact that the true Spirit, the Spirit of God, neither comes from this place nor that, neither can his power be controlled or directed by human authority, but his working is ever from above, from God himself. The work of the Holy Spirit is, so to speak, the breath of God, and his power is evermore in a special sense the immediate power of God. Coming downward, therefore, this mysterious wind passed into the chamber where the disciples were assembled, and filled the room. An ordinary rushing mighty wind would have been felt *outside* the room, and would probably have destroyed the house or injured the inmates, if it had been aimed at any one building; but this heavenly gust filled but did not destroy the room, it blessed but did not overthrow the waiting company.

The meaning of the symbol is that as breath, air, [or] wind is the very life of man, so is the Spirit of God, the life of the spiritual man. By him are we quickened at the first; by him are we kept alive afterwards; by him is the inner life nurtured, and increased, and perfected. The breath of the nostrils of the man of God is the Spirit of God.

This holy breath was not only intended to quicken them, but to invigorate them. What a blessing would a breeze be just now to us who sit in this heavy atmosphere! How gladly would we hail a gust from the breezy Down, or a gale from the open sea! If the winds of earth are so refreshing, what must a wind from Heaven be? That rushing mighty wind soon cleared away all earth-engendered damps and vapors; it aroused the disciples and left them braced up for the further work of the Lord. They took in great draughts of heavenly life; they felt animated, aroused, and bestirred. A sacred enthusiasm came upon them, because they were filled with the Holy Ghost; and, girt with that strength, they rose into a nobler form of life than they had known before.

No doubt this wind was intended to show the irresistible power of the Holy Ghost; for simple as the air is, and mobile and apparently feeble, yet set it in motion, and you feel that a thing of life is among you; make that motion more rapid, and who knows the power of the restless giant who has been awakened. See, it becomes a storm, a tempest, a hurricane, a tornado, a cyclone. Nothing can be more potent than the wind when it is thoroughly roused, and so, though the Spirit of God be despised among men, so much so that they do not even believe in his existence, yet let him work with the fullness of his power, and you will see what he can do. He comes softly, breathing like a gentle zephyr which fans the flowers, but does not dislodge the insect of most gauzy wing, and our hearts are comforted. He comes like a stirring breeze, and we are quickened to a livelier diligence: our sails are hoisted and we fly before the gale. He comes with yet greater strength, and we prostrate ourselves in the dust as we hear the thunder of his power, bringing down with a crash false confidences and refuges of lies! How the firm reliances of carnal men, which seemed to stand like rocks, are utterly cast down! How men's hopes, which appeared to be rooted like oaks, are torn up by the roots before the breath of the convincing Spirit! What can stand against him? Oh! that we did but see in these latter days something of that mighty rushing wind, which breaketh the cedars of Lebanon, and sweeps before it all things that would resist its power.

The second Pentecostal symbol was *fire*. Fire, again, is a frequent symbol of Deity. Abraham saw a burning lamp, and Moses beheld a burning bush. When Solomon had built his holy and beautiful house, its consecration lay in the fire of God descending upon the sacrifice to mark that the Lord was there; for when the Lord had dwelt aforetime in the Tabernacle, which was superseded by the Temple, he revealed himself in a pillar of cloud by day and a pillar of fire by night. "Our God is a consuming fire." Hence the symbol of fire is a fit emblem of God the Holy Spirit. Let us adore and worship him. Tongues of flame sitting on each man's head betoken a personal visitation to the mind and heart of each one of the chosen company. Not to consume them came the fires, for no one was injured by the flaming tongue; to men whom the Lord has prepared for his approach, there is no danger in his visitations. They see God, and their lives are preserved; they feel his fires, and are not consumed. This is the privilege of those alone who have been prepared and purified for such fellowship with God.

The intention of the symbol was to show them that the Holy Spirit would illuminate them, as fire gives light. "He shall lead you into all truth." Henceforth they were to be no more children untrained, but to be teachers in Israel, instructors of the nations whom they were to disciple unto Christ: hence the Spirit of light was upon them. But fire doth more than give light: it inflames; and the flames which sat upon each showed them that they were to be ablaze with love, intense with zeal, burning with self-sacrifice; and that they were to go forth among men to speak not with the chill tongue of deliberate logic, but with burning tongues of passionate pleading, persuading and entreating men to come unto Christ, that they might live. The fire signified inspiration. God was about to make them speak under a divine influence, to speak as the Spirit of God should give them utterance. Oh! blessed symbol, would God that all of us experienced its meaning to the full, and that the tongue of fire did sit upon every servant of the Lord. May a fire burn steadily within to destroy our sin, a holy sacrificial flame to make us whole burnt offerings unto God, a never-dying flame of zeal for God and devotion to the cross.

Note that the emblem was not only fire, but a *tongue of fire;* for God meant to have a speaking church: not a church that would fight with the sword (with that weapon we have nought to do) but a church that should have a sword proceeding *out of its mouth,* whose one weapon should be the proclamation of the gospel of Jesus Christ. I should think from what I know of some preachers, that when they had their Pentecost, the influence sat upon them in the form of tongues of flowers! But the apostolic Pentecost knew not flowers, but flames. What fine preaching we have nowadays! What new thoughts, and poetical turns! This is not the style of the Holy Ghost. Soft and gentle is the flow of smooth speech which tells of the dignity of man, the grandeur of the century, the toning down of all punishment for sin, and the probable restoration of all lost spirits, including the arch-fiend himself. This is the Satanic ministry, subtle as the serpent, bland as his seducing words to Eve.

The Holy Ghost calls us not to this mode of speech. Fire, intensity, zeal, passion: [have these] as much as you will; but as for aiming at effect by polished phrases and brilliant periods—these are fitter for those who would deceive men than for those who would tell them the message of the Most High. The style of the Holy Ghost is one which conveys the truth to the mind in the most forcible manner—it is plain but flaming, simple but consuming. The Holy Spirit has never written a cold period throughout the whole Bible, and never did he speak by a man a lifeless word, but evermore he gives and blesses the tongue of fire.

These, then, are the two symbols; and I should like you carefully to observe how the Holy Spirit teaches us by them.

When he came from the Father to his Son Jesus, it was as a dove. Let peace rest on that dear sufferer's soul through all his days of labor and through the passion which would close them. His anointing is that of peace: he needed no tongue of flame, for he was already all on fire with love.

When the Holy Spirit was bestowed by the Son of God upon his disciples, it was as breath—"He breathed on them and said, 'Receive the Holy Ghost.'" To have life more abundantly is a chief necessity of servants of the Lord Jesus, and therefore thus the Holy Ghost visits us.

Now that we have the Holy Spirit from Christ as our inner life and quickening, he also comes upon us with the intent to use us in blessing others, and this is the manner of his visitation—he comes as the wind, which wafts the words we speak, and as fire which, burns a way for the truth we utter. Our words are now full of life and flame; they are borne by the breath of the Spirit, and they fall like fire-flakes, and set the souls of men blazing with desire after God. If the Holy Spirit shall rest upon me or upon you, or upon any of us, to qualify us for service, it shall be after this fashion—not merely of life for ourselves, but of fiery energy in dealing with others. Come on us even now, O rushing mighty wind and tongue of fire, for the world hath great need. It lies stagnant in the malaria of sin and needs a healing wind; it is shrouded in dreadful night, and needs the flaming torch of truth. There is neither health nor light for it but from thee, O blessed Spirit; come, then, upon it through thy people.

Now put these two symbols together; only mind what you are at. Wind and fire together! I have kept them separate in my discourse hitherto; and you have seen power in each one; what are they together? Rushing mighty wind alone: how terrible! Who shall stand against it? See how the gallant ships dash together, and the monarchs of the forest bow their heads. And fire alone! Who shall stand against it when it devours its prey?

But set wind and fire to work in hearty union! Remember the old city of London. When first the flames began, it was utterly impossible to quench them, because the wind fanned the flame, and the buildings gave way before the fire-torrent. Set the prairie on fire. If a rain-shower falls, and the air is still, the grass may perhaps cease to burn, but let the wind encourage the flame, and see how the devourer sweeps along while the tall grass is licked up by tongues of fire. We have lately read of forests on fire. What a sight!

Hear how the mighty trees are crashing in the flame! What can stand against it! The fire setteth the mountains on a blaze. What a smoke blackens the skies; it grows dark at noon. As hill after hill offers up its sacrifice, the timid imagine that the great day of the Lord has come.

If we could see a spiritual conflagration of equal grandeur, it were a consummation devoutly to be wished. O God, send us the Holy Ghost in this fashion: give us both the breath of spiritual life and the fire of unconquerable zeal, till nation after nation shall yield to the sway of Jesus. O thou who art our God, answer us by fire, we pray thee. Answer us both by wind and fire, and then shall we see thee to be God indeed. The kingdom comes not, and the work is flagging. O that thou wouldest send the wind and the fire! Thou wilt do this when we are all of one accord, all believing, all expecting, all prepared by prayer. Lord, bring us to this waiting state.

II. Secondly, my brethren, follow me while I call your attention to *the immediate effects* of this descent of the Holy Spirit, for these symbols were not sent in vain.

There were two immediate effects: the first was *filling*, and the second was the *gift of utterance*. I call special attention to the first, namely, filling: "It filled all the house where they were sitting": and it did not merely fill the house, but the men—"They were all filled with the Holy Ghost." When they stood up to speak, even the ribald mockers in the crowd noticed this, for they said, "These men are full," and though they added "with new wine," yet they evidently detected a singular fullness about them. We are poor, empty things by nature, and useless while we remain so: we need to be filled with the Holy Ghost. Some people seem to believe in the Spirit of God giving utterance only, and they look upon instruction in divine things as of secondary importance. Dear, dear me, what trouble comes when we act upon that theory! How the empty vessels clatter, and rattle, and sound! Men in such case utter a wonderful amount of nothing, and even when that nothing is set on fire it does not come to much. I dread a revival of that sort, where the first thing and the last thing is everlasting talk. Those who set up for teachers ought to be themselves taught of the Lord; how can they communicate that which they have not received? Where the Spirit of God is truly at work, he first fills and then gives utterance: that is his way. Oh that you and I were at this moment filled with the Holy Ghost. "Full!" Then they were not cold, and dead, and empty of life as we sometimes are. "Full." Then there was no room for anything else in any one of them! They were too completely occupied by the heavenly power to have room for the desires of the flesh. Fear was banished, every minor motive was expelled: the Spirit of God, as it flooded their very being, drove out of them everything that was extraneous. They had many faults and many infirmities before, but that day, when they were filled with the Spirit of God, faults and infirmities were no more perceptible. They became different men from what they had ever been before: men full of God are the reverse of men full of self, The difference between an empty man and a full man is something very wonderful. Let a thirsty person have an empty vessel handed to him. There may be much noise in the handing, but what a mockery it is as it touches his lips. But fill it with refreshing water, and perhaps there may be all the more silence in the passing it, for a full cup needs careful handling; but oh, what a blessing when it reaches the man's lips! Out of a full vessel he may drink his fill. Out of a full church, the world shall receive salvation, but never out of an empty one. The first thing we want as a church is to be filled with the Holy Ghost: the gift of utterance will then come as a matter of course.

They ask me, "May the sisters speak anywhere? If not in the assembly, may they not speak in smaller meetings?" I answer, yes, if they are full of the Holy Ghost. Shall this brother or that be allowed to speak? Certainly, if he be filled, he may flow. May a layman preach? I know nothing about laymen except that I am no cleric myself; but let all speak who are full of the Holy Ghost. "Spring up, O well." If it be a fountain of living water, who would restrain it, who *could* restrain it? Let him overflow who is full, but mind he does not set up to pour out when there is nothing in him; for if he counts it his official duty to go pouring out, pouring out, pouring out, at unreasonable length, and yet nothing comes of it, I am sure he acts, not by the Holy Spirit, but according to his own vanity.

The next Pentecostal symbol was *utterance*. As soon as the Spirit of God filled them, they began to speak at once. It seems to me that they began to speak before the people had come together. They could not help it; the inner forces demanded expression, and they must speak. So when the Spirit of God really comes upon a man, he does not wait till he has gathered an audience of the size which he desires, but he seizes the next opportunity. He speaks to one person, he speaks to two, he speaks to three, to anybody: he must speak, for he is full, and must have vent.

When the Spirit of God fills a man, he speaks so as to be understood. The crowd spake different languages, and these Spirit-taught men spoke to them in the language of the country in which they were born. This is one of the signs of the Spirit's utterance. If my friend over yonder talks in a Latinized style to a company of costermongers [street venders], I will warrant you the Holy Ghost has nothing to do with him. If a learned brother fires over the heads of his congregation with a grand oration, he may trace his elocution, if he likes, to Cicero and Demosthenes, but do not let him ascribe it to the Holy Spirit, for that is not after His manner. The Spirit of God speaks so that his words may be understood, and if there be any obscurity, it lies in the language used by the Lord himself. The crowd not only understood, but they felt. There were lancets in this Pentecostal preaching, and the hearers "were pricked in the heart." The truth wounded men, and the slain of the Lord were many, for the wounds were in the most vital part. They could not make it out: they had heard speakers before, but this was quite a different thing. The men spake fire-flakes, and one hearer cried to his fellow, "What is this?" The preachers were speaking flame, and the fire dropped into the hearts of men till they were amazed and confounded.

Those are the two effects of the Holy Spirit: a fullness of the Spirit in the ministry and the church; and next, a fire ministry, and a church on fire, speaking so as to be felt and understood by those around. Causes produce effects like themselves, and this wind and fire ministry soon did its work. We read that this "was noised abroad." Of course it was, because there had been a noise as of a rushing mighty wind. Next to that we read that all the people came together, and were confounded. There was naturally a stir, for a great wind from Heaven was rushing. All were amazed and astonished, and while some enquired believingly, others began to mock. Of course they did: there was a fire burning, and fire is a dividing thing, and this fire began to separate between the precious and the vile, as it always will do when it comes into operation. We may expect at the beginning of a true revival to observe a movement among the people, a noise, and a stir. These things are not done in a corner. Cities will know of the presence of God, and crowds will be attracted by the event.

This was the immediate effect of the Pentecostal marvel, and I shall now ask you to follow me to my third point, which is this:

III. The Holy Spirit being thus at work, *what was the most prominent subject which these full men began to preach about, with words of fire?*

Suppose that the Holy Spirit should work mightily in the church, what would our ministers preach about? We should have a revival, should we not, of the old discussions about predestination and free agency? I do not think so: these are happily ended, for they tended towards bitterness, and for the most part the disputants were not equal to their task. We should hear a great deal about the pre-millennial and the post-millennial advent, should we not? I do not think so. I never saw much of the Spirit of God in discussions or dreamings upon times and seasons which are not clearly revealed. Should we not hear learned essays upon advanced theology? No, sir; when the devil inspires the church, we have modern theology; but when the Spirit of God is among us, that rubbish is shot out with loathing.

What did these men preach about? Their hearers said, "We do hear them speak in our own tongues the wonderful works of God." Their subject was the *wonderful works of God*. Oh, that this might be, to my dying day, my sole and only topic—"The wonderful works of God." For, first, they spoke of *redemption,* that wonderful work of God. Peter's sermon was a specimen of how they spoke of it. He told the people that Jesus was the Son of God, that they had crucified and slain him, but that he had come to redeem men, and that there was salvation through his precious blood. He preached redemption! Oh, how this land will echo again and again with "Redemption, redemption, redemption,

redemption by the precious blood," when the Holy Ghost is with us. This is fit fuel for the tongue of flame: this is something worthy to be wafted by the divine wind. "God was in Christ, reconciling the world unto himself, not imputing their trespasses unto them." "The blood of Jesus Christ his Son cleanseth us from all sin." This is one of the wonderful works of God of which we can never make too frequent mention.

They certainly spoke of the next wonderful work of God, namely, *regeneration*. There was no concealing of the work of the Holy Spirit in that primitive ministry. It was brought to the front. Peter said, "Ye shall receive the Holy Ghost." The preachers of Pentecost told of the Spirit's work by the Spirit's power: conversion, repentance, renewal, faith, holiness, and such things were freely spoken of and ascribed to their real author, the divine Spirit. If the Spirit of God shall give us once again a full and fiery ministry, we shall hear it clearly proclaimed, "Ye must be born again," and we shall see a people forthcoming which are born, not of blood, nor of the will of the flesh, but of the will of God, and by the energy which cometh from Heaven. A Holy Ghost ministry cannot be silent about the Holy Ghost and his sacred operations upon the heart.

And very plainly they spoke on a third wonderful work of God, namely, *remission of sin*. This was the point that Peter pushed home to them, that on repentance they should receive remission of sins. What a blessed message is this—pardon for crimes of deepest dye, a pardon bought with Jesus' blood, free pardon, full pardon, irreversible pardon given to the vilest of the vile when they ground their weapons of rebellion, and bow at the feet that once were nailed to the tree. If we would prove ourselves to be under divine influence, we must keep to the divine message of fatherly forgiveness to returning prodigals. What happier word can we deliver?

These are the doctrines which the Holy Ghost will revive in the midst of the land when he worketh mightily—redemption, regeneration, remission. If you would have the Spirit of God resting on your labors, dear brothers and sisters, keep these three things ever to the front, and make all men hear in their own tongue the wonderful works of God.

IV. I shall close by noticing, in the fourth place, what were the *glorious results* of all this.

Have patience with me, if you find the details somewhat long. The result of the Spirit coming as wind and fire—filling and giving utterance—was, first, in the hearers' *deep feeling*. There was never, perhaps, in the world such a feeling excited by the language of mortal man as that which was aroused in the crowds in Jerusalem on that day. You might have seen a group here, and a group there, all listening to the same story of the wondrous works of God, and all stirred and affected; for the heavenly wind and fire went with the preaching, and they could not help feeling its power. We are told that they were pricked in the heart. They had painful emotions, they felt wounds which killed their enmity. The word struck at the center of their being: it pierced the vital point. Alas, people come into our places of worship nowadays to hear the preacher, and their friends ask them on their return, "How did you like him?" Was that your errand, to see how you *liked* him? What practical benefit is there in such a mode of using the servants of God? Are we sent among you to give opportunities for criticism? Yet the mass of men seem to think that we are nothing better than fiddlers or play-actors, who come upon the stage to help you while away an hour. O my hearers, if we are true to our God, and true to you, ours is a more solemn business than most men dream. The object of all true preaching is the heart: we aim at divorcing the heart from sin, and wedding it to Christ. Our ministry has failed, and has not the divine seal set upon it, unless it makes men tremble, makes them sad, and then anon brings them to Christ, and causes them to rejoice. Sermons are to be heard in thousands, and yet how little comes of them all, because the heart is not aimed at, or else the archers miss the mark. Alas, our hearers do not present their hearts as our target, but leave them at home, and bring us only their ears, or their heads. Here we need the divine aid. Pray mightily that the Spirit of God may rest upon all who speak in God's name, for then they will create deep feeling in their hearers!

Then followed an *earnest enquiry*. "They were pricked in their heart, and they said to Peter and the rest of the apostles, 'Men and brethren, what shall we do?'" Emotion is of itself but a poor result unless it leads to practical action. To make men feel is well enough, but it must be a feeling which impels them to immediate movement, or at least to earnest enquiry as to what they shall do. O Spirit of God, if thou wilt rest on me, even me, men shall not hear and go their way and forget what they have heard! They will arise and seek the Father, and taste his love. If thou wouldst rest on all the brotherhood that publish thy word, men would not merely weep while they hear, and be affected while the discourse lasts, but they would go their way to ask, "What must we do to be saved?" This is what we need. We do not require new preachers, but we need anew anointing of the Spirit. We do not require novel forms of service, but we want the fire Spirit, the wind Spirit to work by us till everywhere men cry, "What must we do to be saved?"

Then came a *grand reception of the word*. We are told that they gladly received the word, and they received it in two senses: first, Peter bade them *repent*, and so they did. They were pricked to the heart from compunction on account of what they had done to Jesus, and they sorrowed after a godly sort, and quitted their sins. They also *believed* in him whom they had slain, and accepted him as their Savior there and then, without longer hesitancy. They trusted in him whom God had set forth to be a propitiation, and thus they fully received the word. Repentance and faith make up a complete reception of Christ and they bad both of these. Why should we not see this divine result today? We shall see it in proportion to our faith.

But what next? Why, they were *baptized* directly. Having repented and believed, the next step was to make confession of their faith; and they did not postpone that act for a single day; why should they? Willing hands were there, the whole company of the faithful were all glad to engage in the holy service, and that same day were they baptized into the name of the Father, and of the Son, and of the Holy Spirit. If the Holy Ghost were fully with us, we should never have to complain that many believers never confess their faith, for they would be eager to confess the Savior's name in his own appointed way. Backwardness to be baptized comes too often of fear of persecution, indecision, love of ease, pride, or disobedience; but all these vanish when the heavenly wind and fire are doing their sacred work. Sinful diffidence soon disappears, sinful shame of Jesus is no more seen, and hesitancy and delay are banished for ever when the Holy Spirit works with power.

Furthermore, there was not merely this immediate confession, but as a result of the Spirit of God, there was *great steadfastness*. "They continued steadfastly in the apostles' doctrine." We have had plenty of revivals of the human sort, and their results have been sadly disappointing. Under excitement, nominal converts have been multiplied: but where are they after a little testing? I am sadly compelled to own that, so far as I can observe, there has been much sown, and very little reaped that was worth reaping, from much of that which has been called revival. Our hopes were flattering as a dream; but the apparent result has vanished like a vision of the night. But where the Spirit of God is really at work, the converts stand: they are well rooted and grounded, and hence they are not carried about by every wind of doctrine, but they continue steadfast in the apostolic truth.

We see next that there was *abundant worship of God,* for they were steadfast not only in the doctrine, but in breaking of bread, and in prayer, and in fellowship. There was no difficulty in getting a prayer meeting then, no difficulty in maintaining daily communion then, no want of holy fellowship then; for the Spirit of God was among them, and the ordinances were precious in their eyes. "Oh," say some, "if we could get this minister or that evangelist, we should do well." Brothers, if you had the *Holy Spirit,* you would have everything else growing out of his presence, for all good things are summed up in him.

Next to this, there came *striking generosity*. Funds were not hard to raise: liberality overflowed its banks, for believers poured all that they had into the common fund. Then was it indeed seen to be true that the silver and the gold are the Lord's. When the Spirit of God operates powerfully, there is little need to issue telling appeals for widows and orphans, or to go down on your knees and plead for missionary fields which cannot be occupied for want of money. At this moment, our village churches can scarcely support their pastors at a starvation rate; but I believe that if the Spirit of God will visit all the churches, means will be forthcoming to keep all going right vigorously. If this does not happen, I tremble for our Nonconformist churches, for the means of their existence will be absent; both as to spiritual and temporal supplies, they will utterly fail. There will be no lack of money when there is no lack of grace. When the Spirit of God comes, those who have substance yield it to their Lord: those who have but little, grow rich by giving of that little, and those who are already rich become happy by consecrating what they have. There is no need to rattle the box when the rushing mighty wind is heard, and the fire is dissolving all hearts in love.

Then came *continual gladness.* "They did eat their meat with gladness." They were not merely glad at prayer-meetings and sermons, but glad at breakfast and at supper. Whatever they had to eat, they were for singing over it. Jerusalem was the happiest city that ever was when the Spirit of God was there. The disciples were singing from morning to night, and I have no doubt the outsiders asked, "What is it all about?" The temple was never so frequented as then; there was never such singing before; the very streets of Jerusalem, and the Hill of Zion, rang with the songs of the once despised Galileans.

They were full of gladness, and that gladness showed itself in praising God. I have no doubt they broke out now and then in the services with shouts of, "Glory! Hallelujah!" I should not wonder but what all propriety was scattered to the winds. They were so glad, so exhilarated, that they were ready to leap for joy. Of course we never say "Amen," or "Glory!" now. We have grown to be so frozenly proper that we never interrupt a service in any way, because, to tell the truth, we are not so particularly glad, we are not so specially full of praise, that we want to do anything of the sort. Alas, we have lost very much of the Spirit of God, and much of the joy and gladness which attend his presence, and so we have settled into a decorous apathy! We gather the pinks [flowers] of propriety instead of the palm branches of praise. God send us a season of glorious disorder. Oh, for a sweep of wind that will set the seas in motion, and make our ironclad brethren now lying so quietly at anchor to roll from stem to stern. As for us, who are as the little ships, we will fly before the gale if it will but speed us to our desired haven. Oh, for fire to fall again—fire which shall affect the most stolid! This is a sure remedy for indifference. When a flake of fire falls into a man's bosom, he knows it, and when the word of God comes home to a man's soul, he knows it too. Oh that such fire might first sit upon the disciples, and then fall on all [those] around!

For, to close, there was then a *daily increase* of the church—"The Lord added to the church daily such as should be saved." Conversion was going on perpetually; additions to the church were not events which happened once a year, but they were everyday matters, "so mightily grew the word of God and prevailed."

O Spirit of God, thou art ready to work with us today even as thou didst then! Stay [delay] not, we beseech thee, but work at once. Break down every barrier that hinders the incoming of thy might. Overturn, overturn, O sacred wind! Consume all obstacles, O heavenly fire, and give us now both hearts of flame and tongues of fire to preach thy reconciling word, for Jesus' sake. Amen.

The Indwelling and Outflowing of the Holy Spirit

Delivered on Lord's Day morning, May 28, 1882, at the Metropolitan Tabernacle, Newington. No. 1662.

He that believeth on me, as the scripture hath said, out of his belly shall flow rivers of living water. (But this spake he of the Spirit, which they that believe on him should receive: for the Holy Ghost was not yet given; because that Jesus was not yet glorified.)—John 7:38–39

Nevertheless I tell you the truth; it is expedient for you that I go away: for if I go not away, the Comforter will not come unto you; but if I depart, I will send him unto you.—John 16:7

It is essential, dear friends, that we should worship the living and true God. It will be ill for us if it can be said, "Ye worship ye know not what." "Thou shalt worship the Lord thy God, and him only shalt thou serve." The heathen err from this command by multiplying gods, and making this and that image to be the object of their adoration. Their excess runs to gross superstition and idolatry. I fear that sometimes we who "profess and call ourselves Christians" err in exactly the opposite direction. Instead of worshipping *more* than God, I fear we worship *less* than God. This appears when we forget to pay due adoration to the Holy Spirit of God. The true God is triune: Father, Son, and Holy Spirit; and though there be but one

God, yet that one God has manifested himself to us in the trinity of his sacred persons. If then, I worship the Father and the Son, but forget or neglect to adore the Holy Spirit, I worship less than God. While the poor heathen, in his ignorance, goes far beyond and transgresses, I must take care lest I fall short and fail too. What a grievous thing it will be if we do not pay that loving homage and reverence to the Holy Spirit which is so justly his due. May it not be the fact that we enjoy less of his power and see less of his working in the world because the church of God has not been sufficiently mindful of him? It is a blessed thing to preach the work of Jesus Christ, but it is an evil thing to omit the work of the Holy Ghost; for the work of the Lord Jesus itself is no blessing to that man who does not know the work of the Holy Spirit. There is the ransom price, but it is only through the Spirit that we know the redemption: there is the precious blood, but it is as though the fountain had never been filled, unless the Spirit of God lead us with repenting faith to wash therein. The bandage is soft and the ointment is effectual, but the wound will never be healed till the Holy Spirit shall apply that which the great Physician has provided. Let us not therefore be found neglectful of the work of the divine Spirit, lest we incur guilt, and inflict upon ourselves serious damage.

You that are believers have the most forcible reasons to hold the Holy Ghost in the highest esteem; for what are you now without him? What were you, and what would you still have been, if it had not been for his gracious work upon you? He quickened you, else you had not been in the living family of God today. He gave you understanding that you might know the truth, else would you have been as ignorant as the carnal world is at this hour. It was he that awakened your conscience, convincing you of sin: it was he that gave you abhorrence of sin, and led you to repent: it was he that taught you to believe, and made you see that glorious Person who is to be believed, even Jesus, the Son of God. The Spirit has wrought in you your faith and love and hope, and every grace. There is not a jewel upon the neck of your soul which he did not place there.

> *For every virtue we possess,*
> *And every victory won,*
> *And every thought of holiness,*
> *Are his alone.*

What have we learned—if we have learned aright—except by the teaching of the Holy Ghost? What can we say either in prayer to God or in teaching to men that shall be acceptable, unless we receive the unction of the Holy One of Israel? Brethren, who is it that has comforted us in our distresses, directed us in our perplexities, strengthened us in our weaknesses, and helped our infirmities in ten thousand ways? Is it not the Comforter whom the Father hath sent in Jesus' name? Can I speak too highly of the riches of his grace toward us? Can I too much extol the love of the Spirit? I know I cannot, and you that know what he has wrought in you, delight to hear him highly spoken of and his work and offices set forth. We are bound by a thousand ties to seek his honor who has wrought in us our salvation. Let us never grieve him by our ingratitude, but let us endeavor to extol him. For my part, it shall be the labor of this morning to impress upon you the necessity for his work, and the superlative value of it.

Beloved brethren, notwithstanding all that the Spirit of God has already done in us, it is very possible that we have missed a large part of the blessing which he is willing to give, for he is able to "do exceeding abundantly above all that we ask or think." We have already come to Jesus, and we have drunk of the life-giving stream: our thirst is quenched, and we are made to live in him. Is this all? Now that we are living in him, and rejoicing to do so, have we come to the end of the matter? Assuredly not. We have reached as far as that first exhortation of the Master, "If any man thirst, let him come unto me and drink": but do you think that the generality of the church of God have ever advanced to the next, "He that believeth on me, as the Scripture hath said, out of his belly shall flow rivers of living water"? I think I am not going beyond the grievous truth if I say that only here and there will you find men and women who have believed up to that point. Their thirst is quenched, as I have said, and they live, and because Jesus lives, they shall live also; but health and vigor they have not—they have life, but they have not life more abundantly. They have little life with which to act upon others: they have no energy welling up and overflowing to go streaming out of them like rivers. They have not thought it possible, perhaps, or thinking it possible they have not imagined it possible to themselves; or believing it possible to themselves, they have not aspired to it, but they have stopped short of the fullest blessing. Their wading in to the sacred river has contented them, and they know nothing of "waters to swim in." Like the Israelites of old, they are slow to possess all the land of promise, but sit down when the war has hardly begun. Brothers, let us go in to get of God all that God will give us: let us set our heart upon this, that we mean to have by God's help all that the infinite goodness of God is ready to bestow. Let us not be satisfied with the sip that saves, but let us go on to the baptism which buries the flesh and raises us in the likeness of the risen Lord: even that baptism into the Holy Ghost and into fire which makes us spiritual and sets us all on flame with zeal for the glory of God and eagerness for usefulness by which that glory may be increased among the sons of men.

Thus I introduce you to my texts, and by their guidance we will enter upon the further consideration of the operations of the Holy Spirit, especially of those to which we would aspire.

I. We will commence with the remark that *the work of the Spirit is intimately connected with the work of Christ.*

It is a great pity when persons preach the Holy Spirit's work so as to obscure the work of Christ; and I have known some do that, for they have held up before the sinner's eye the inward experience of believers, instead of lifting up first and foremost the crucified Savior, to whom we must look and live. The gospel is not "Behold the Spirit of God" but "Behold the Lamb of God." It is an equal pity when Christ is so preached that the Holy Spirit is ignored; as if faith in Jesus prevented the necessity of the new birth, and *imputed* righteousness rendered *imparted* righteousness needless. Have I not often reminded you that in the third chapter of John—where Jesus taught Nicodemus the doctrine, "Except a man be born again of water and of the spirit, he cannot enter the kingdom of Heaven,"—we also read those blessed words,

> And as Moses lifted up the serpent in the wilderness, even so must the Son of man be lifted up: that whosoever believeth in him should not perish, but have eternal life. For God so loved the world, that he gave his only begotten Son, that whosoever believeth in him should not perish, but have everlasting life.

The necessity for regeneration by the Spirit is there put very clearly, and so is the free promise that those who trust in Jesus shall be saved. This is what we ought to do: we must take care to let both these truths stand out most distinctly—with equal prominence. They are intertwined with each other and are necessary, each to each: what God hath joined together, let no man put asunder.

They are so joined together that, first of all, *the Holy Spirit was not given until Jesus had been glorified.* Carefully note our first text; it is a very striking one: "This spake he out of the Spirit, which they that believe on him should receive, for the Holy Ghost was not yet." The word "given" is not in the original: it is inserted by the translators to help out the sense, and they were perhaps wise in making such an addition, but the words are more forcible by themselves. How strong the statement, "For the Holy Ghost was not yet." Of course, we none of us dream that the Holy Spirit was not yet existing, for he is eternal and self-existent, being most truly God, but he was not yet in fellowship with man to the full extent in which he now is, since Jesus Christ is glorified. The near and dear intercourse of God with man which is expressed by the indwelling of the Spirit could not take place till redeeming work was done and the Redeemer was exalted. As far as men were concerned, and the fullness of the blessing was concerned, indicated by the outflowing rivers of living water, the Spirit of God was not yet.

"Oh," say you, "but was not the Spirit of God in the church in the wilderness, and with the saints of God in all former ages?" I answer, "Certainly, but not in the manner in which the Spirit of God now resides in the church of Jesus Christ."

You read of the prophets, and of one and another gracious man, that the Spirit of God came upon them, seized them, moved them, spake by them; but he did not *dwell* in them. His operations upon men were a coming and a going: they were carried away by the Spirit of God, and came under his power, but the Spirit of God did not rest upon them or abide in them. Occasionally the sacred endowment of the Spirit of God came upon them, but they knew not "the communion of the Holy Ghost." As a French pastor very sweetly puts it,

> He appeared *unto* men; he did not incarnate himself *in* man. His action was intermittent: he went and came, like the dove which Noah sent forth from the ark, and which went to and fro, finding no rest; while in the new dispensation he *dwells*— he abides in the heart, as the dove, his emblem, which John the Baptist saw descending and alighting upon the head of Jesus. Affianced of the soul, the Spirit went off to see his betrothed, but was not yet one with her; the marriage was not consummated until the Pentecost, after the glorification of Jesus Christ.

You know how our Lord puts it, "He dwelleth with you, and shall be in you." That indwelling is another thing from being *with* us. The Holy Spirit was *with* the Apostles in the days when Jesus was with them; but he was not *in* them in the sense in which he filled them at and after the Day of Pentecost. The operations of the Spirit of God before our Lord's ascension were not according to the full measure of the gospel, but now the Spirit of God has been poured upon us from on high; now he has descended, and now he abides in the midst of the church, and now we enter into him and are baptized into the Holy Ghost, while he enters into us and makes our bodies to be his temples. Jesus said, "I will send you another Comforter, which shall abide with you forever;" not coming and going, but remaining in the midst of the church. This shows how intimately the gift of the Holy Ghost is connected with our Lord Jesus Christ, inasmuch as in the fullest sense of his indwelling the Holy Ghost could not be with us until Christ had been glorified. It has been well observed that our Lord sent out seventy evangelists to preach the gospel, even as he had aforetime sent out the twelve; and no doubt they preached with great zeal and produced much stir; but the Holy Ghost never took the trouble to preserve one of their sermons, or even the notes of one. I have not the slightest doubt that they were very crude and incomplete, showing more of human zeal than of divine unction, and hence they are forgotten; but no sooner had the Holy Spirit fallen than Peter's first sermon is recorded, and henceforth we have frequent notes of the utterances of apostles, deacons, and evangelists. There was an abiding fullness, and an overflowing of blessing, out of the souls of the saints after the Lord was glorified, which was not existing among men before that time.

Observe, too, that the Holy Spirit was given after the ascent of our divine Lord into his glory, partly *to make that ascent the more renowned*. When he ascended up on high, he led captivity captive and gave gifts to men. These gifts were men in whom the Holy Spirit dwelt, who preached the gospel unto the nations. The shedding of the Holy Spirit upon the assembled disciples on that memorable day was the glorification of the risen Christ upon the earth. I know not in what way the Father could have made the glory of Heaven so effectually to flow from the heights of the New Jerusalem and to come streaming down among the sons of men as by giving that chief of all gifts—the gift of the Holy Spirit, when the Lord had risen and gone into his glory. With emphasis, may I say of the Spirit at Pentecost, that he glorified Christ by descending at such a time. What grander celebration could there have been? Heaven rang with hosannas, and earth echoed the joy. The descending Spirit is the noblest testimony among men to the glory of the ascended Redeemer.

Was not the Spirit of God also sent at that time as *an evidence of our divine Master's acceptance?* Did not the Father thus say to the church, "My Son has finished the work, and has fully entered into his glory, therefore give I you of the Holy Spirit"? If you would know what a harvest is to come of the sowing of the bloody sweat and of the death wounds, see the first fruits. Behold how the Holy Spirit is given, himself to be the first fruits, the earnest of the glory which shall yet be revealed in us. I want no better attestation from God of the finished work of Jesus than this blazing, flaming seal of tongues of fire upon the heads of the disciples. He must have done his work, or such a boon as this would not have come from it.

Moreover, if you desire to see how the work of the Spirit comes to us in connection with the work of Christ, *recollect that it is the Spirit's work to bear witness of Jesus Christ.* He does not take of a thousand different matters and show them to us, but he shall take "of mine," saith Christ, "and he shall show them unto you." The Spirit of God is engaged in a service in which the Lord Jesus Christ is the beginning and the end. He comes to men that they may come to Jesus. Hence he comes to convince us of sin, that he may reveal the great sacrifice of sin: he comes to convince us of righteousness, that we may see the righteousness of Christ; and of judgment, that we may be prepared to meet him when he shall come to judge the quick and dead. Do not think that the Spirit of God has come or ever will come among us to teach us a new gospel, or something other than is written in the Scriptures. Men come to me with their fudges and fancies, and tell me that they were revealed to them by the Holy Spirit. I abhor their blasphemous impertinence, and refuse to listen to them for a minute. They tell me this and that absurdity, and then father it upon the Spirit of wisdom. It is enough to try our patience to hear their foolish ravings but to find the Holy Spirit charged with them is more than we can bear. We have tests and judgments by which to know whether they who claim to speak by the Holy Spirit do so or not: for the testimony of the Spirit is ever most honorable to our Lord Jesus Christ, and does not concern itself with the trifles of time and the follies of the flesh.

It is by the gospel of Jesus Christ that the Spirit of God works in the hearts of men. "Faith cometh by hearing, and hearing by the word of God": the Holy Spirit uses the hearing of the word of God for the conviction, conversion, consolation, and sanctification of men. His usual and ordinary method of operation is to fasten upon the mind the things of God, and to put life and force into the consideration of them. He revives in men's memories things that have long been forgotten, and he frequently makes these the means of affecting the heart and conscience. The men can hardly recollect hearing these truths, but still they were heard by them at some time or other. Saving truths are such matters as are contained in their substance in the word of God, and lie within the range of the teaching, or the person, or work, or offices of our Lord Jesus Christ. It is the Spirit's one business here below to reveal Christ to us and in us, and to that work he steadily adheres.

Moreover, *the Holy Spirit's work is to conform us to the likeness of Jesus Christ*. He is not working us to this or that human ideal, but he is working us into the likeness of Christ, that he may be the first-born among many brethren. Jesus Christ is that standard and model to which the Spirit of God by his sanctifying processes is bringing us till Christ be formed in us the hope of glory.

Evermore it is for the glory of Jesus that the Spirit of God works. He works not for the glory of a church or of a community: he works not for the honor of a man or for the distinction of a sect: his one great object is to glorify Christ. "He shall glorify me" is our Savior's declaration, and when he takes of the things of Christ and shows them unto us, we are led more and more to reverence and love and adore our blessed Lord Jesus Christ.

I will not detain you longer with this. You will see how the works of Jesus and of the Spirit are joined together indissolubly, so that we may neither set the work of Jesus before the work of the Spirit, nor the work of the Spirit before the work of Jesus, but we are glad to joy in both and to make much of them. As we delight in the Father's love and the grace of our Lord Jesus, so do we equally rejoice in the communion of the Holy Ghost, and these three agree in one.

II. We will now advance another step, and here we shall need our second text. *The operations of the Holy Spirit are of incomparable value.*

They are of such incomparable value that the very best thing we can think of was not thought to be so precious as these are. Our Lord himself says, "It is expedient for you that I go away: for if I go not away, the Comforter will not come unto you." Beloved friends, the presence of Jesus Christ was of inestimable value to his disciples, and yet it was not such an advantage to his servants as the indwelling of the Holy Spirit. Is not this a wonderful statement? Well might our Lord preface it by saying, "Now I tell you the truth," as if he felt that they would find it a hard saying, for a hard saying it is. Consider for a moment what Christ was to his disciples while he was here, and then see what must be the value of the Spirit's operations when it is expedient that they should lose all that blessing in order to receive the Spirit of God. Our Lord Jesus Christ was to them their teacher—they had learned everything from his lips. He was their leader—they had never to ask what to do, they had only to follow in his steps. He was their defender— whenever the Pharisees or Sadducees assailed them he was like a brazen wall to them. He was their comforter—in all times of grief they resorted to him, and his dear sympathetic heart poured out floods of comfort at once. What if I were to say that the Lord Jesus Christ was everything to them, their all in all? What a father is to his children, ay, what a mother is to her suckling, that was Jesus Christ to his disciples; and yet the Spirit of God's abiding in the church is better even than all this.

Now take another thought. What would you think if Jesus Christ were to come among us now as in the days of his flesh. I mean, not as he will come, but as he appeared at his first advent. What joy it would give you! Oh, the delights, the heavenly joys, to hear that Jesus Christ of Nazareth was on earth again, a man among men! Should we not clap our hands for joy? Our one question would be, "Master, where dwellest thou?" For we should all long to live just where he lived. We could then sympathize with the blacks when they flocked into Washington in large numbers to take up their residence there [after the Civil War]. Why, think you, did they come to live in that city? Because Massa Abraham Lincoln lived there, who had set them free, and they thought it would be glorious to live as near as possible to their great friend. If Jesus lived anywhere—it would not matter where, if it were in the desert or on the bleakest of mountains—there would be a rush to the place. How would the spot be crowded! What rents they would pay for the worst of tenements if Jesus was but in the neighborhood! But do you not see the difficulty? We could not all get near him in any literal or corporeal fashion. Now that the church is multiplied into millions of believers, some of the Lord's followers would never be able to see him, and the most could only hope to speak with him now and then. In the days of his flesh, the twelve might see him every day, and so might the little company of disciples, but the case is altered now that multitudes are trusting in his name.

If our Lord were at this time living in the United States, we should be much grieved to have an ocean between us and our leader. All the companies that could be formed would not be able to run enough boats to carry us over. If the Master personally came here to this little island, it would not hold all the vast company of the faithful who would flock to it. It is much better to have the Holy Spirit, because he is dwelling *with* us and *in* us. The difficulties of the bodily presence are too great, and so, though we would be thankful, like the apostles, if we had known Christ after the flesh, yet we do not marvel that they expressed little sorrow when they said that, after the flesh they knew even him no more. The Comforter had filled the void caused by his absence, and made them rejoice, because the Lord had gone unto his Father.

Are we not apt to think that if our Lord Jesus were here, it would give unspeakable strength to the church? Would not the enemy be convinced if they saw him? No, they would not. If they hear not Moses and the prophets, neither would they be converted, though one rose from the dead. Jesus rose, but they did not therefore believe. If our Lord had lingered here all this while, his personal presence would not have converted unbelievers, for nothing can do that but the power of the Holy Ghost.

"But," you say, "surely it would thrill the church with enthusiasm." Fancy the Lord himself standing on this platform this morning in the same garb as when he was upon earth. Oh, what rapturous worship! What burning zeal! What enthusiasm! We should go home in such a state of excitement as we never were in before. Yes, it is even so, but then the Lord is not going to carry on his kingdom by the force of mere mental excitement, not even by such enthusiasm as would follow the sight of his person. The work of the Holy Spirit is a truer work, a deeper work, a surer work, and will more effectually achieve the purposes of God than even would the enthusiasm to which we should be stirred by the bodily presence of our well-beloved Savior. The work is to be spiritual, and therefore the visible presence has departed. It is better that it should be so. We must walk by faith, and by faith alone—how could we do this if we could see the Lord with these mortal eyes? This is the dispensation of the unseen Spirit, in which we render glory to God by trusting in his word and relying upon the unseen energy. Now, faith works, and faith triumphs, though the world seeth not the foundation upon which faith is built, for the Spirit who works in us cannot be discerned by carnal minds—the world seeth him not, neither knoweth him.

Thus you see that the operations of the Holy Spirit must be inestimably precious. There is no calculating their value, since it is expedient that we lose the bodily presence of Christ rather than remain without the indwelling of the Spirit of God.

III. Now go back to my first text again, and follow me in the third head.

Those operations of the Spirit of God, of which I am afraid some Christians are almost ignorant, are of wondrous power. The text says, "He that believeth on me, out of the midst of him shall flow rivers of living water." *These operations are of marvellous power.* Brethren, do you understand my text? Do rivers of living water flow out of you?

Notice, first, that this is to be an inward work: the rivers of living water are to flow out of the midst of the man. The words are according to our version, "Out of his belly"—that is, from his heart and soul. The rivers do not flow out of his mouth: the promised power is not oratory. We have had plenty of words, floods of words; but this is *heart* work. The source of the rivers is found in the inner life. It is an inward work at its fountain head. It is not a work of talent, and ability, and show, and glitter, and glare: it is altogether an inward work. The life-flood is to come out of the man's inmost self, out of the bowels and essential being of the man. Homage is shown too generally to outward form and external observance, though these soon lose their interest and power. But when the Spirit of God rests within a man, it exercises a home rule [self-government] within him, and he gives great attention to what an old divine was wont to call "the home department." Alas, many neglect the realm within, which is the chief province under our care. O my brother in Christ, if you would be useful, begin with yourself. It is out of your very soul that a blessing must come. It cannot come out of you if it is not in you: and it cannot be in you unless God the Holy Ghost places it there.

Next, *it is life-giving work*. Out of the heart of the man, out of the center of his life, are to flow rivers of living water; that is to say, he is instrumentally to communicate to others the divine life. When he speaks, when he prays, when he acts; he shall so speak and pray and act that there shall be going out of him an emanation [emission] which is full of the life of grace and godliness. He shall be a light by which others shall see. His life shall be the means of kindling life in other men's bosoms. "Out of his belly shall flow rivers of living water."

Note *the plenitude of it*. The figure would have been a surprising one if it had said, "Out of him shall flow a *river* of living water"; but it is not so: it says *rivers*. Have you ever stood by the side of a very abundant spring? We have some such not far from London. You see the water bubbling up from many little mouths. Observe the sand dancing as the water forces its way from the bottom; and there, just across the road, a mill is turned by the stream which has just been created by the spring, and when the waterwheel is turned you see a veritable river flowing forward to supply Father Thames [River]. Yet this is only one river; what would you think if you saw a spring yielding such supplies that a river flowed from it to the north, and a river to the south, a river to the east, and a river to the west? This is the figure before us: rivers of living water flowing out of the living man in all directions. "Ah," say you, "I have not reached to that." A point is gained when you know, confess, and deplore your failure. If you say, "I have all things and abound," I am afraid you will never reach the fullness of the blessing; but if you know something of your failure, the Lord will lead you further. It may be that the spirit of life which comes forth of you is but a trickling brooklet, or even a few tiny drops; then be sure to confess it, and you will be on the way to a fuller blessing. What a word is this! *Rivers of living water!!* Oh, that all professing Christians were such fountains.

See how *spontaneous* it is: "Out of the midst of him shall flow." No pumping is required; nothing is said about machinery and hydraulics; the man does not want exciting and stirring up, but, just as he is, influence of the best kind quietly flows away from him. Did you ever hear a great hubbub in the morning, a great outcry, a sounding of trumpets and drums, and did you ever ask, "What is it?" Did a voice reply, "The sun is about to rise, and he is making this noise that all may be aware of it"? No, he shines, but he has nothing to say about it; even so the genuine Christian just goes about flooding the world with blessing, and so far from claiming attention for himself, it may be that he himself is unconscious of what he is effecting. God so blesses him that his leaf does not wither, and whatsoever he doeth is prospering, for he is like a tree planted by the rivers of water that bringeth forth its fruit in its season: his verdure [greenery] and fruit are the natural outcome of his vigorous life. Oh, the blessed spontaneity of the work of grace when a man gets into the fullness of it, for then he seems to eat and drink and sleep eternal life, and he spreads a savor of salvation all round.

And this is to be perpetual—not like intermittent springs which burst forth and flow in torrents, and then cease—but it is to be an everyday outgushing. In summer and winter, by day and by night, wherever the man is, he shall be a blessing. As he breathes, he shall breathe benedictions; as he thinks, his mind shall be devising generous things; and when he acts, his acts shall be as though the hand of God were working by the hand of man.

I hope I hear many sighs rising up in the place! I hope I hear friends saying, "Oh, that I could get to that." I want you to attain the fullness of the favor. I pray that we may all get it; for, because Jesus Christ is glorified, therefore the Holy Spirit is given in this fashion, given more largely to those in the kingdom of Heaven than to all those holy men before the Lord's ascent to his glory. God gives no stinted blessing to celebrate the triumph of his Son: God giveth not the Spirit by measure [in limited amounts] unto him. On such an occasion, Heaven's grandest liberality was displayed. Christ is glorified in Heaven above, and God would have him glorified in the church below by vouchsafing a baptism of the Holy Ghost to each of us.

So I close by this, which I hope will be a very comforting and inspiring reflection.

IV. *These operations of the Spirit of God are easily to be obtained by the Lord's children.*

Did you say you had not received them? They are to be had, they are to be had at once. First, they are to be had *by believing in Jesus.* "This spake he of the Spirit, which they that believe on him should receive." Do you not see that it is faith which gives us the first drink and causes us to live, and this second more abundant blessing, of being ourselves made fountains from which rivers flow, comes in the same way? Believe in Christ, for the blessing is to be obtained, not by the works of the law, nor by so much of fasting, and striving, and effort, but by belief in the Lord Jesus, for it. With him is the residue of the Spirit. He is prepared to give this to you, aye, to every one of you who believe on his name. He will not, of course, make all of you preachers; for who then would be hearers? If all were preachers, the other works of the church would be neglected; but he will give you this favor, that out of you there shall stream a divine influence all round you to bless your children, to bless your servants, to bless the workmen in the house where you are employed, and to bless the street you live in. In proportion, as God gives you opportunity these rivers of living water will flow in this channel and in that, and they will be pouring forth from you at all times, if you believe in Jesus for the full blessing, and can by faith receive it.

But there is another thing to be done as well, and that is *to pray;* and here I want to remind you of those blessed words of the Master,

> Everyone that asketh receiveth; and he that seeketh findeth; and to him that knocketh it shall be opened. If a son shall ask bread of any of you that is a father, will he give him a stone? Or if he ask a fish, will he for a fish give him a serpent? Or if he shall ask an egg, will he offer him a scorpion? If ye then, being evil, know how to give good gifts unto your children: how much more shall your heavenly Father give the Holy Spirit to them that ask him?

You see, there is a distinct promise to the children of God, that their heavenly Father will give them the Holy Spirit if they ask for his power; and that promise is made to be exceedingly strong by the instances joined to it. If there be a promise that God can break (which there is not), this is not the promise, for God has put it in the most forcible and binding way. I know not how to show you its wonderful force. Did you ever hear of a man who, when his child asked for bread, gave him a stone? Go to the worst part of London, and will you find a man of that kind? You shall, if you like, get among pirates and murderers, and when a little child cries, "Father, give me a bit of bread and meat," does the most wicked father fill his own little one's mouth with stones? Yet the Lord seems to say that this is what he would be doing if he were to deny us the Holy Spirit when we ask him for his necessary working: he would be like one that gave his children stones instead of bread. Do you think the Lord will ever bring himself down to that? But he says, *"How much more* shall your heavenly Father give the Holy Spirit to them that ask him?" He makes it a stronger case than that of an ordinary parent. The Lord must give us the Spirit when we ask him, for he has herein bound himself by no ordinary pledge. He has used a simile which would bring dishonor on his own name, and that of the very grossest kind, if he did not give the Holy Spirit to them that ask him.

Oh, then, let us ask him at once, with all our hearts. Am I not so happy as to have in this audience some who will immediately ask? I pray that some who have never received the Holy Spirit at all may now be led, while I am speaking, to pray, "Blessed Spirit, visit me; lead me to Jesus." But especially those of you that are the children of God—to you is this promise especially made. Ask God to make you all that the Spirit of God can make you, not only a satisfied believer who has drunk for himself, but a useful believer, who overflows the neighborhood with blessing. I see here a number of friends from the country who have come to spend their holiday in London. What a blessing it would be if they went back to their respective churches overflowing; for there are numbers of churches that need flooding; they are dry as a barn-floor, and little dew ever falls on them. Oh, that they might be flooded! What a wonderful thing a flood is! Go down to the river, look over the bridge, and see the barges and other craft lying in the mud. All the king's horses and all the king's men cannot tug them out to sea. There they lie, dead and motionless as the mud itself. What shall we do with them? What machinery can move them? Have we a great engineer among us who will devise a scheme for lifting these vessels and bearing them down to the river's month? No, it cannot be done. Wait till the tide comes in! What a change! Each vessel walks the water like a thing of life. What a difference between the low tide and the high tide. You cannot stir the boats when the water is gone; but when the tide is at the full, see how readily they move; a little child may push them with his hand. Oh, for a flood of grace. The Lord send to all our churches a great springtide! Then the indolent will be active enough, and those who were half dead will be full of energy. I know that in this particular dock, several vessels are lying that I should like to float, but I cannot stir them. They neither work for God nor come out to the prayer-meetings, nor give of their substance to spread the gospel. If the flood would come, you would see what they are capable of: they would be active, fervent, generous, abounding in every good word and work. So may it be! So may it be! May springs begin to flow in all our churches, and may all of you who hear me this day get your share of the streams! Oh, that the Lord may now fill you and then send you home bearing a flood of grace with you. It sounds oddly to speak of a man's carrying home a flood within him, and yet I hope it will be so, and that out of you shall flow rivers of living water. So may God grant, for Jesus' sake. Amen.

The Abiding of the Spirit Is the Glory of the Church

Delivered on Lord's Day morning, September 5, 1886, at the Metropolitan Tabernacle, Newington. No. 1918.

"Yet now be strong, O Zerubbabel," saith the Lord; "and be strong, Joshua, son of Josedech, the high priest, and be strong, all ye people of the land," saith the Lord, "and work: for I am with you," saith the Lord of hosts: "according to the word that I covenanted with you when ye came out of Egypt, so my spirit remaineth among you: fear ye not."—Haggai 2:4–5

Satan is always doing his utmost to stay the work of God. He hindered these Jews from building the temple, and today he endeavors to hinder the people of God from spreading the gospel. A spiritual temple is to be built for the Most High, and if by any means the evil one can delay its uprising, he will stick at nothing: if he can take us off from working with faith and courage for the glory of God he will be sure to do it. He is very cunning, and knows how to change his argument and yet keep to his design: little cares he how he works, so long as he can hurt the cause of God. In the case of the Jewish people on their return from captivity, he sought to prevent the building of the temple by making them selfish and worldly, so that every man was eager to build his own house, and cared nothing for the house of the Lord. Each family pleaded its own urgent needs. In returning to a long-deserted and neglected land, much had to be done to make up for lost time; and to provide suitably for itself, every family needed all its exertions. They carried this thrift and self-providing to a great extreme, and secured for themselves luxuries, while the foundations of the temple which had been laid years before remained as they were, or became still more thickly covered up with rubbish. The people could not be made to bestir themselves to build a house of God, for they answered to every exhortation, "The time is not come, the time that the Lord's house should be built." A more convenient season was always looming in the future, but it never came. Just now it was too hot, further on it was too cold; at one time the wet season was just setting in, and it was of no use to begin, and soon after the fair weather required that they should be in their own fields. Like some in our day, they saw to themselves first, and God's turn was very long in coming; hence the prophet cried, "Is it time for you, O ye, to dwell in your ceiled [roofed] houses, and this house lie waste?"

By the mouth of his servant Haggai, stern rebukes were uttered, and the whole people were aroused. We read in verse twelve of the first chapter,

> Then Zerubbabel the son of Shealtiel, and Joshua the son of Josedech, the high priest, with all the remnant of the people, obeyed the voice of the Lord their God, and the words of Haggai the prophet, as the Lord their God had sent him, and the people did fear before the Lord.

All hands were put to the work; course after course of stone began to rise; and then another stumbling-block was thrown in the way of the workers. The older folks remarked that this was a very small affair compared with the temple of Solomon, of which their fathers had told them; in fact, their rising building was nothing at all, and not worthy to be called a temple.

The prophet describes the feeling in the verse which precedes our text.

> Who is left among you that saw this house in her first glory? And how do ye see it now? Is it not in your eyes in comparison of it as nothing?

Feeling that their work would be very poor and insignificant, the people had little heart to go on. Being discouraged by the humiliating contrast, they began to be slack; and as they were quite willing to accept any excuse (and here was an excuse ready made for them) they would soon have been at a standstill had not the prophet met the wiles of the arch-enemy with another word from the Lord. Nothing so confounds the evil one as the voice of the Eternal. Our Lord himself defeated Satan by the word of the Lord; and the prophet Haggai did the same. The subtle craft of the enemy is defeated by the wisdom of the Most High, which reveals itself in plain words of honest statement. The Lord cuts the knots which bind his people, and sets them at liberty to do his will. He did this by assuring them that he was with them. Twice the voice was heard—*"I am with you, saith the Lord of hosts."* They were also assured that what they built was accepted, and that the Lord meant to fill the new house with glory; yea, he meant to light it up with a glory greater than that which honored the temple of Solomon. They were not spending their strength for nought, but were laboring with divine help and favor. Thus they were encouraged to put their shoulders to the work: the walls rose in due order, and God was glorified in the building up of his Zion.

The present times are, in many respects, similar to those of Haggai. History certainly repeats itself within the church of God as well as outside of it; and therefore the messages of God need to be repeated also. The words of some almost-forgotten prophet may be re-delivered by the watchman of the Lord in these present days, and be a timely word for the present emergency. We are not free from the worldliness which puts self first and God nowhere, else our various enterprises would be more abundantly supplied with the silver and the gold which are the Lord's, but which even professing Christians reserve for themselves. When this selfish greed is conquered, then comes in a timorous depression. Among those who have escaped from worldliness, there is apt to be too much despondency, and men labor feebly as for a cause which is doomed to failure. This last evil must be cured. I pray that our text may this morning came from the Lord's own mouth with all the fire which once blazed about it. May faint hearts be encouraged and drowsy spirits be aroused, as we hear the Lord say, *"My Spirit remaineth among you: fear ye not."*

I shall enter fully upon the subject, by the assistance of the Holy Spirit, by calling your attention to *discouragement forbidden*. Then I shall speak of *encouragement imparted*, and, having done so, I shall linger with this blessed text, which overflows with comfort, and shall speak, in the third place, of *encouragement further applied*. Oh that our Lord, who knows how to speak a word in season to him that is weary, may cheer the hearts of seekers by what shall be spoken under this last head of discourse!

I. To begin with, here is *discouragement forbidden*.

Discouragement comes readily enough to us poor mortals who are occupied in the work of God, seeing it is a work of faith, a work of difficulty, a work above our capacity, and a work much opposed.

Discouragement as very natural: it is a native of the soil of manhood. To believe is supernatural, faith is the work of the Spirit of God; to doubt is natural to fallen men; for we have within us an evil heart of unbelief. It is abominably wicked, I grant you; but still it is natural, because of the downward tendency of our depraved hearts. Discouragement towards good things is a weed that grows without sowing. To be faint-hearted and downcast happens to some of us when we are half drowned in this heavy atmosphere, and it also visits us on the wings of the east wind. It takes little to make some hands hang down: a word or a look will do it. I do not, therefore, excuse it; but the rather I condemn myself for having a nature prone to such evil.

Discouragement may come and does come to us, as it did to these people, from a consideration of the great things which God deserves at our hands, and the small things which we are able to render. When in Haggai's days the people thought of Jehovah, and of a temple for him, and then looked upon the narrow space which had been enclosed, and the common stones which had been laid for foundations, they were ashamed. Where were those hewn stones and costly stones which, of old, Solomon brought from afar? They said within themselves, "This house is unworthy of Jehovah: what do we by laboring thus?" Have you not felt the depressing weight of what is so surely true? Brethren, all that we do is little for our God; far too little for him that loved us and gave himself for us. For him that poured out his soul unto death on our behalf, the most splendid service, the most heroic self-denial, are all too little; and we feel it is so. Alabaster boxes of precious ointment are too mean a gift. It does not occur to our fervent spirit to imagine that there can be any waste when our best boxes are broken and the perfume is poured out lavishly for him. What we do fear is that our alabaster boxes are too few, and that our ointment is not precious enough. When we have done our utmost in declaring the glory of Jesus, we have felt that words are too poor and mean to set forth our adorable Lord.

When we have prayed for his kingdom, we have been disgusted with our own prayers; and all the efforts we have put forth in connection with any part of his service have seemed too few, too feeble for us to hope for acceptance. Thus have we been discouraged. The enemy has worked upon us by this means, yet he has made us argue very wrongly. Because we could not do much, we have half-resolved to do nothing! Because what we did was so poor, we were inclined to quit the work altogether! This is evidently absurd and wicked. The enemy can use humility for his purpose as well as pride. Whether he makes us think too much or too little of our work, it is all the same to him, so long as he can get us off from it.

It is significant that the man with one talent went and hid his Lord's money in the earth. He knew that it was but one, and for that reason he was the less afraid to bury it. Perhaps he argued that the interest on one talent could never come to much, and would never be noticed side by side with the result of five or ten talents; and he might as well bring nothing at all to his Lord as bring so little. Perhaps he might not have wrapped it up if it had not been so small that a napkin could cover it. The smallness of our gifts may be a temptation to us. We are consciously so weak and so insignificant, compared with the great God and his great cause, that we are discouraged, and think it vain to attempt anything.

Moreover, the enemy contrasts our work with that of others, and with that of those who have gone before us. We are doing so little as compared with other people, therefore let us give up. We cannot build like Solomon, therefore let us not build at all. Yet, brethren, there is a falsehood in all this, for, in truth, nothing is worthy of God. The great works of others, and even the amazing productions of Solomon, all fell short of His glory. What house could man build for God? What are cedar, and marble, and gold as compared with the glory of the Most High? Though the house was "exceeding magnifical," yet the Lord God had of old dwelt within curtains, and never was his worship more glorious than within the tent of badgers' skins; indeed, as soon as the great house was built, true religion declined. What of all human work can be worthy of the Lord? Our little labors do but share the insignificance of greater things, and therefore we ought not to withhold them: yet here is the temptation from which we must pray to be delivered.

The tendency to depreciate the present because of the glories of the past is also injurious. The old people looked back to the days of the former temple, even as we are apt to look upon the times of the great preachers of the past. What work was done in those past days! What Sabbaths were enjoyed then! What converts were added to the church! What days of refreshing were then vouchsafed! Everything has declined, decreased, degenerated! As for the former days, they beheld a race of giants, who are now succeeded by pigmies. We look at one of these great men, and cry,

> Why, man, he doth bestride the narrow world
> Like a Colossus; and we petty men
> Walk under his huge legs, and peep about
> To find ourselves dishonorable graves.

But, brethren, we must not allow this sense of littleness to hamper us; for God can bless our littleness, and use it for his glory. I notice that the great men of the past thought of themselves even as we think of ourselves. Certainly they were not more self-confident than we are. I find in the stories of the brave days of old, the same confessions and the same lamentations which we utter now. It is true that in spiritual strength we are not what our fathers were; I fear that Puritanic holiness and truthfulness of doctrine are dying out, while adherence to principle is far from common; but our fathers had also faults and follies to mourn over, and they did mourn over them most sincerely.

Instead of being discouraged because what we do is unworthy of God, and insignificant compared with what was done by others, let us gather up our strength to reform our errors, and reach to higher attainments. Let us throw our heart and soul into the work of the Lord, and yet do something more nearly in accordance with our highest ideal of what our God deserves of us. Let us excel our ancestors. Let us aspire to be even more godly, more conscientious, and more sound in the faith than they were, for the Spirit of God remaineth with us.

Brethren, it is clear that discouragement can be produced by these reasons, and yet they are a mere sample of a host of arguments which work in the same direction: hence *discouragement is very common*. Haggai was sent to speak to Zerubbabel, the governor, and to Joshua, the high priest, and to all the remnant of the people. The great man may become discouraged: he that leads the van [troops] has his fainting fits; even Elijah cries, "Let me die!" The consecrated servant of God, whose life is a priesthood, is apt to grow discouraged, too: standing at God's altar, he sometimes trembles for the ark of the Lord. The multitude of the people are all too apt to suffer from panic, and to flee at the sight of the enemy. How many are they who say, "The old truth cannot succeed: the cause of orthodoxy is desperate; we had better yield to the modern spirit!"

This faint-heartedness is so common that it has been the plague of Israel from her first day until now. They were discouraged at the Red Sea, at the mere rattling of Pharaoh's chariots; they were discouraged when they found no water; they were discouraged when they had eaten up the bread which they brought out of Egypt; they were discouraged when they heard of the giants, and of the cities walled to Heaven. I need not lengthen the wretched catalogue. What has not cowardice done? The fearful and unbelieving have brought terrible disasters upon our camps. Discouragement is the national epidemic of our Israel. "Being armed and carrying bows," we turn back in the day of battle. This is as common among Christians as consumption[1] among the inhabitants of this foggy island. Oh that God would save us all from distrust, and cause us to [a]quit ourselves like men!

Wherever discouragement comes in, it is dreadfully weakening. I am sure it is weakening, because the prophet was bidden to say three times to the governor, high priest, and people, "Be strong." This proves that they had become weak. Being discouraged, their hands hung down, and their knees were feeble. Faith girds us with omnipotence; but unbelief makes everything hang loose and limp about us. Distrust, and thou wilt fail in everything; believe, and according to thy faith so shall it be unto thee.

To lead a discouraged people to the Holy War is as difficult as [it was] for Xerxes' commanders to conduct the Persian troops to battle against the Greeks. The vassals of the great king were driven to the conflict by whips and sticks, for they were afraid to fight: do you wonder that they were defeated? A church that needs constant exhorting and compelling accomplishes nothing. The Greeks had no need of blows and threats, for each man was a lion, and courted the encounter, however great the odds against him. Each Spartan fought *con amore* [with zeal]; he was never more at home than when contending for the altars and the hearths of his country. We want Christian men of this same sort, who have faith in their principles, faith in the doctrines of grace, faith in God the Father, God the Son, and God the Holy Ghost, and who therefore contend earnestly for the faith in these days when piety is mocked at from the pulpit, and the gospel is sneered at by professional preachers. We need men who love the truth, to whom it is dear as their lives; men into whose hearts the old doctrine is burned by the hand of God's Spirit

---

[1] Consumption: archaic term for pulmonary tuberculosis.

through a deep experience of its necessity and of its power. We need no more of those who will parrot what they are taught, but we want men who will speak what they know. Oh, for a troop of men like John Knox, heroes of the martyr and covenanter stock! Then would Jehovah of hosts have a people to serve him who would be strong in the Lord and in the power of his might.

Discouragement not only weakens men, but it *takes them off from the service of God*. It is significant that the prophet said to them, "'Be strong, all ye people of the land,' saith the Lord, 'and work.'" They had ceased to build: they had begun to talk and argue, but they had laid down the trowel. They were extremely wise in their observations, and criticisms, and prophecies; but the walls did not rise. One person knew exactly how big the former temple was; another declared that their present architect was not up to the mark, and that the structure was not built in a scientific manner: one objected to this, and another to that; but everybody was wiser than all the rest, and sneered at old-fashioned ways. It is always so when we are discouraged: we cease from the work of the Lord, and waste time in talk and nonsensical refinements. May the Lord take away discouragement from any of you who now suffer from it! I suppose some of you do feel it, for at times it creeps over my heart and makes me go with heaviness to my work.

I believe that God's truth will come to the front yet, but it hath many adversaries today. All sorts of unbeliefs are being hatched out from under the wings of "modern thought." The gospel seems to be regarded as a nose of wax, to be altered and shaped by every man who wishes to show his superior skill. Nor is it in doctrine alone, but in practice also, that the times are out of joint. Separateness from the world, and holy living, are to give place to gaiety and theater-going. To follow Christ fully has gone out of fashion with many of those from whom we once hoped better things. Yet are there some who waver not, some who are willing to be in the right, with two or three [others]. For my own part, even should I find none around me of the same mind, I shall not budge an inch from the old truth, nor sweat a hair for fear of its overthrow; but I shall abide confident that the eternal God, whose truth we know and hold, will vindicate himself ere long, and turn the wisdom of the world into babble, and its boasting into confusion. Blessed is the man who shall be able to stand fast by his God in these evil days. Let us not in any wise be discouraged. "Be strong; be strong; be strong," sounds as a threefold voice from the triune God. "Fear not" comes as a sweet cordial to the faint: therefore let no man's heart fail him. Thus much about the discouragement.

II. Secondly, here is *the encouragement imparted,* which is the grand part of our text.

"According to the word that I covenanted with you when ye came out of Egypt, so my spirit remaineth among you: fear ye not." God remembers his covenant and stands to his ancient promises. When the people came out of Egypt the Lord was with them by his Spirit: hence he spoke to them by Moses, and through Moses he guided, and judged, and taught them. He was with them also by his Spirit in inspiring Bezaleel and Aholiab as to the works of art which adorned the tabernacle. God always finds workmen for his work, and by his Spirit fits them for it. The Spirit of God rested upon the elders who were ordained to relieve Moses of his great burden. The Lord was also with his people in the fiery cloudy pillar which was conspicuous in the midst of the camp. His presence was their glory and their defense.

This is a type of the presence of the Spirit with the church. At the present day, if we hold the truth of God, if we live in obedience to his holy commands, if we are spiritually minded, if we cry unto God in believing prayer, if we have faith in his covenant and in his Son, the Holy Spirit abideth among us. The Holy Ghost descended upon the church at Pentecost, and he has never gone back again: there is no record of the Spirit's return to Heaven. He will abide with the true church evermore. This is our hope for the present struggle. The Spirit of God remaineth with us.

To what end, my brethren, is this Spirit with us? Let us think of this, that we may be encouraged at this time. The Spirit of God remaineth among you to aid and assist the ministry which he has already given. Oh, that the prayers of God's people would always go up for God's ministers, that they may speak with a divine power and influence which none shall be able to gainsay! We look too much for clever men; we seek out fluent and flowery speakers; we sigh for men cultured and trained in all the knowledge of the heathen: nay, but if we sought more for unction, for divine authority, and for that power which doth hedge about [surround] the man of God, how much wiser should we be! Oh, that all of us who profess to preach the gospel would learn to speak in entire dependence upon the direction of the Holy Spirit, not daring to utter our own words, but even trembling lest we should do so, and committing ourselves to that secret influence, without which nothing will be powerful upon the conscience or converting to the heart. Know ye not the difference between the power that cometh of human oratory, and that which cometh by the divine energy which speaks so to the heart that men cannot resist it? We have forgotten this too much. It were better to speak six words in the power of the Holy Ghost than to preach seventy years of sermons without the Spirit. He who rested on those who have gone to their reward in Heaven can rest this day upon our ministers and bless our evangelists, if we will but seek it of him. Let us cease to grieve the Spirit of God, and look to him for help to the faithful ministers who are yet spared to us.

This same Spirit who of old gave to his church eminent teachers can raise up other and more useful men. The other day, a brother from Wales told me of the great men he remembered: he said that he had never heard such a one as Christmas Evans,[2] who surpassed all men when he was in the hwyl. I asked him if he knew another Welsh minister who preached like Christmas Evans. "No," he said, "we have no such man in Wales in our days." So in England we have neither Wesley nor Whitefield, nor any of their order; yet, as with God is the residue of the Spirit, he can fetch out from some chimney-corner another Christmas Evans, or find in our Sunday-school another George Whitefield, who shall declare the gospel with the Holy Ghost sent down from Heaven. Let us never fear for the future, or despair for the present, since the Spirit of God remaineth with us. What if the growing error of the age should have silenced the last tongue that speaks out the old gospel? Let not faith be weakened. I hear the tramp of legions of soldiers of the cross. I hear the clarion voices of hosts of preachers. "The Lord give the word; great was the company of those that published it." Have faith in God through our Lord Jesus Christ! When he ascended on high he led captivity captive, and received gifts for men. He then gave apostles, teachers, preachers, and evangelists, and he can do the like again. Let us fall back upon the eternal God, and never be discouraged for an instant.

Nor is this all. The Holy Spirit being with us, *he can move the whole church to exercise its varied ministries.* This is one of the things we want very much—that every member of the church should recognize that he is ordained to service. Everyone in Christ, man or woman, hath some testimony to bear, some warning to give, some deed to do in the name of the holy child Jesus; and if the Spirit of God be poured out upon our young men and our maidens, each one will be aroused to energetic service. Both small and great will be in earnest, and the result upon the slumbering masses of our population will surprise us all. Sometimes we lament that the churches are so dull. There is an old proverb which says of So-and-so, that he was "as sound asleep as a church." I suppose there is nothing that can sleep so soundly as a church. But yet the Spirit of God still remaineth, and therefore churches go to be awakened. I mean that not only in part but as a whole, a church may be quickened. The dullest professor, the most slovenly believer, the most captious and useless member of a church, may yet be turned to good account. I see them like a stack of faggots, piled up, dead, and dry. Oh for the fire! We will have a blaze out of them yet.

Come, Holy Spirit, heavenly Dove, brood over the dark, disordered church as once thou didst over chaos, and order shall come out of confusion, and the darkness shall fly before the light. Only let the Spirit be with us, and we have all that is

---

[2] Christmas Evans (1766-1838) was a Welsh Nonconformist divine born near the village of Llandyssul, Cardiganshire, on the 25th of December 1766. His father, a shoemaker, died early, and the boy grew up as an illiterate farm laborer. (Wikipedia.com)

wanted for victory. Give us his presence, and everything else will come in its due season for the profitable service of the entire church.

If the Spirit be with us, there will come multitudinous conversions. We cannot get at "the lapsed masses," as they are pedantically called. We cannot stir the crass infidelity of the present age: no, we cannot, but *He* can. All things are possible with God. If you walk down to our bridges [on the Thames River] at a certain hour of the day you will see barges and vessels lying in the mud; and all the king's horses and all the king's men cannot stir them. Wait until the tide comes in, and they will walk the water like things of life. The living flood accomplishes at once what no mortals can do. And so today our churches cannot stir. What shall we do? Oh, that the Holy Spirit would come with a flood-tide of his benign influences, as he will if we will but believe in him; as he must if we will but cry unto him; as he shall if we will cease to grieve him. Everything will be even as the saints desire when the Lord of saints is with us. The hope of the continuance and increase of the church lies in the remaining of the Spirit with us. The hope of the salvation of London lies in the wonder-working Spirit. Let us bow our heads and worship the omnipotent Spirit who deigns to work *in* us, *by* us, and *with* us.

Then, brethren, if this should happen—and I see not why it should not—then we may expect to see the Church put on her beautiful garments; then shall she begin to clear herself of the errors which now defile her; then shall she press to her bosom the truths which she now begins to forget; then will she go back to the pure fount of inspiration and drink from the Scriptures of truth; and then out of the midst of her shall flow no turbid streams, but rivers of living water. If the Holy Ghost will work among us, we shall rejoice in the Lord, and glory in the name of our God.

When once the Spirit of God putteth forth his might, all things else will be in accord with him. Notice that in the rest of the chapter—which I shall read now, not as relating to that temple at all, but to the church of God—there is great comfort given to us. If the Holy Spirit be once given, then we may expect providence to co-operate with the church of God. Read verse 6:

> Yet once, it is a little while, and I will shake Heaven and the earth, and the sea, and the dry land. I will shake all nations.

Great commotions will co-operate with the Holy Spirit. We may expect that God will work for his people in an extraordinary fashion if they will but be faithful to him. Empires will collapse, and times will change, for the truth's sake. Expect the unexpected, reckon upon that which is unlikely, if it be necessary for the growth of the kingdom. Of old the earth helped the woman when the dragon opened his mouth to drown her with the floods that he cast forth: unexpected help shall come to us when affairs are at their worst.

Specially do I look for a shaking among the hosts of unbelief. How often did the Lord of old rout his enemies without his Israel drawing sword! The watchword was, "Stand ye still, and see the salvation of the Lord." The adversaries of old fell out among themselves; and they will do so again. When Cadmus slew the dragon with his javelin, he was bidden to sow its teeth in the earth. When he did so, according to the classic fable, he saw rising out of the ground nodding plumes, and crested helmets, and broad shoulders of armed men. Up from the earth there sprang a host of warriors; but Cadmus needed not to fly; for the moment they found their feet, these children of the dragon fell upon each other till scarcely one was left. Error, like Saturn, devours its own children. Those that fight against the Lord of hosts are not agreed among themselves; they shall sheathe their swords in each other's bosoms.

I saw in the night vision the sea, the deep and broad sea of truth, flashing with its silver waves. Lo, a black horse came out of the darkness and went down to the deep, threatening to drink it dry. I saw him stand there drinking, and swelling as he drank. In his pride he trusted that he could snuff up Jordan at a draught. I stood by and saw him drink, and then plunge further into the sea, to drink still more. Again he plunged in with fury, and soon he lost his footing, and I saw him no more, for the deep had swallowed him that boasted that he would swallow it. Rest assured that every black horse of error that comes forth to swallow up the sea of divine truth shall be drowned therein. Wherefore be of good courage. God, who maketh the earth and the heavens to shake, shall cause each error to fall like an untimely fig.

And next, the Lord in this chapter promises his people that they shall have all the supplies they need for his work. They feared that they could not build his house, because of their poverty; but, saith the Lord of hosts, "The silver and the gold are mine." When the church of God believes in God, and goes forward bravely, she need not trouble as to supplies. Her God will provide for her. He that gives the Holy Ghost will give gold and silver according as they are needed; therefore let us be of good courage. If God is with us, why need we fear? One of our English kings once threatened the great city of London that if its councilors talked so independently, he would—yes—he would, indeed he would—take his court away from the city. The Lord Mayor on that occasion replied, that if his majesty would graciously leave the river Thames behind him, the citizens would try to get on without his court. If any say, "If you hold to these old-fashioned doctrines, you will lose the educated, the wealthy, the influential," we answer, "But if we do not lose the godly and the presence of the Holy Ghost, we are not in the least alarmed." If the Holy Ghost remaineth with us, there is a river, the streams whereof make glad the city of God. Brethren, my heart leaps within me as I cry, "The Lord of hosts is with us; the God of Jacob is our refuge." "Therefore will not we fear, though the earth be removed, and though the mountains be carried into the midst of the sea."

The best comfort of all remained: "The desire of all nations shall come." This was in a measure fulfilled when Jesus came into that latter house and caused all holy hearts to sing for gladness; but it was not wholly fulfilled in that way; for if you notice, in the ninth verse it is written, "The glory of this latter house shall be greater than of the former; and in this place will I give peace," which the Lord did not fully do to the second temple, since that was destroyed by the Romans. But there is another advent, when "the desire of all nations shall come" in power and glory; and this is our highest hope. Though truth may be driven back, and error may prevail, Jesus comes, and he is the great Lord and patron of truth: he shall judge the world in righteousness, and the people in equity. Here's our last resource; here are God's reserves. He whom we serve liveth and reigneth forever and ever; and he saith, "Behold, I come quickly; and my reward is with me, to give every man according as his work shall be." "Therefore, my beloved brethren, be ye steadfast, unmovable, always abounding in the work of the Lord, forasmuch as ye know that your labor is not in vain in the Lord."

III. I should have [been] done if it had not been that this text seemed to me to overflow so much, that it might not only refresh God's people, but give drink to thirsty sinners who are seeking the Lord. For a moment or two I give myself to *encouragement further applied.*

It is at the beginning of every gracious purpose that men have most fear, even as these people had who had newly begun to build. When first the Holy Spirit begins to strive with a man and to lead him to Jesus, he is apt to say—"I cannot; I dare not; it is impossible. How can I believe and live?"

Now I want to speak to some of you here who are willing to find Christ, and to encourage you by the truth that the Spirit lives to help you. I would even like to speak to those who are not anxious to be saved. I remember that Dr. Payson, an exceedingly earnest and useful man of God, once did a singular thing. He had been holding inquiry meetings with all sorts of people, and great numbers had been saved. At last, one Sunday he gave out that he should have a meeting on Monday night of those persons who did not desire to be saved; and, strange to say, some twenty persons came who did not wish to repent or believe. He spoke to them and said,

> I am sure that if a little film, thin as the web of the gossamer, were let down by God from Heaven to each one of you, you would not push it away from you. Although it were almost invisible, you would value even the slightest connection between you and Heaven. Now, your coming to meet me tonight is a little link with God. I want it to increase in strength till you are joined to the Lord forever.

He spoke to them most tenderly, and God blessed those people who did not desire to be saved, so that before the meeting was over, they were of another mind. The film had become a thicker thread, and it grew and grew until the Lord Christ held them by it forever. Dear friends, the fact of your being in the Tabernacle[3] this morning is like that filmy thread: do not put it away. Here is your comfort: the Holy Spirit still works with the preaching of the word.

Do I hear you say, "I cannot feel my need of Christ as I want to feel it?" The Spirit remaineth among us. He can make you feel more deeply the guilt of sin and your need of pardon.

"But I have heard so much about conviction and repentance; I do not seem to have either of them." Yet the Spirit remaineth with us, and that Spirit is able to work in you the deepest conviction and the truest repentance.

"O sir, I do not feel as if I could do anything:" but the Spirit remaineth with us, and all things that are needful for godliness, he can give. He can work in you to will and to do of his own good pleasure.

"But I want to believe in the Lord Jesus Christ unto eternal life." Who made you want to do that? Who but the Holy Spirit? Therefore he is still at work with you; and though as yet you do not understand what believing is (or else I am persuaded you would believe at once), the Spirit of God can instruct you in it. You are blind, but he can give you sight; you are paralyzed, but he can give you strength—the Spirit of God remaineth.

"Oh, but that doctrine of regeneration staggers me: you know, we must be born again." Yes, we are born again of the Spirit, and the Spirit remaineth still with us; he is still mighty to work that wondrous change, and to bring you out of the kingdom of Satan into the kingdom of God's dear Son. The Spirit remaineth with us, blessed be his name.

"Ah, dear sir," says one, "I want to conquer sin!" Who made you desire to conquer sin? Who, but the Spirit that remaineth with us? He will give you the sword of the Spirit and teach you how to use it, and he will give you both the will and the power to use it successfully. Through the Spirit's might, you can overcome every sin, even that which has dragged you down and disgraced you. The Spirit of God is still waiting to help you. When I think of the power of the Spirit of God, I look hopefully upon every sinner here this morning. I bless his name that he can work in you all that is pleasing in his sight. Some of you may be very careless, but he can make you thoughtful. Coming up to London to see the Exhibition, I hope you may yourselves become an exhibition of divine grace. You think not about things, but he can make you feel at this moment a sweet softness stealing over you, until you long to be alone and to get home to the old arm-chair and there seek the Lord. You can thus be led to salvation.

---

[3] Tabernacle: Metropolitan Tabernacle, Spurgeon's church.

I thought when I came in here that I should have a picked congregation; and so I have. You are one of them. Wherever you come from, I want you now to seek the Lord. He has brought you here, and he means to bless you. Yield yourselves to him while his sweet Spirit pleads with you. While the heavenly wind softly blows upon you, open wide every window. You have not felt that you wanted it, but that is the sure proof that you need it; for he who does not know his need of Christ, is most in need. Open wide your heart, that the Spirit may teach you your need; above all, breathe the prayer that he would help you this morning to look to the Lord Jesus Christ, for "there is life in a look at the Crucified One—there is life at this moment for you."

"Oh," you say, "if I were to begin I should not keep on." No; if *you* began, perhaps you would not; but if *he* begins with you he will keep on. The final perseverance of saints is the result of the final perseverance of the Holy Spirit; he perseveres to bless, and we persevere in receiving the blessing. If he begins, you have begun with a divine power that fainteth not neither is weary. I wish it might so happen that on this fifth day of the ninth month, not the prophet Haggai, but I, God's servant, may have spoken to you such a word as you shall never forget; and may the Lord add to the word, by the witness of the Holy Ghost, "From this day will I bless you!" Go away with that promise resting upon you. I would like to give a shake of the hand to every stranger here this morning, and say, "Brother, in the name of the Lord I wish you from this day a blessing." Amen and amen.

The Covenant Promise of the Spirit

Delivered on Lord's Day morning, April 10, 1891, at the Metropolitan Tabernacle, Newington. No. 2200.

And I will put my spirit within you.—Ezekiel 36:27

No preface is needed; and the largeness of our subject forbids our wasting time in beating about the bush. I shall try to do two things this morning: first, I would commend the text; and, secondly, I would in some measure expound the text.

I. First, as for *the commendation of the text,* the tongues of men and of angels might fail.

To call it a golden sentence would be much too commonplace: to liken it to a pearl of great price would be too poor a comparison. We cannot feel, much less speak, too much in praise of that great God who has put this clause into the covenant of his grace. In that covenant every sentence is more precious than Heaven and earth; and this line is not the least among his choice words of promise: "I will put my spirit within you."

I would begin by saying that *it is a gracious word*. It was spoken to a graceless people, to a people who had followed "their own way," and refused the way of God; a people who had already provoked something more than ordinary anger in the Judge of all the earth; for he himself said (verse 18), "I poured my fury upon them." These people, even under chastisement, caused the holy name of God to be profaned among the heathen whither they went. They had been highly favored, but they abused their privileges, and behaved worse than those who never knew the Lord. They sinned wantonly, willfully, wickedly, proudly and presumptuously; and by this they greatly provoked the Lord. Yet to them he made such a promise as this—"I will put my spirit within you." Surely, where sin abounded, grace did much more abound.

Clearly this is a word of grace, for the law saith nothing of this kind. Turn to the law of Moses, and see if there be any word spoken therein concerning the putting of the Spirit within men to cause them to walk in God's statutes. The law proclaims the statutes; but the gospel alone promises the spirit by which the statutes will be obeyed. The law commands and makes us know what God requires of us; but the gospel goes further, and inclines us to obey the will of the Lord, and enables us practically to walk in his ways. Under the dominion of grace, the Lord worketh in us to will and to do of his own good pleasure.

So great a boon as this could never come to any man by merit. A man might so act as to deserve a reward of a certain kind, in measure suited to his commendable action; but the Holy Spirit can never be the wage of human service: the idea verges upon blasphemy. Can any man deserve that Christ should die for him? Who would dream of such a thing? Can any man deserve that the Holy Ghost should dwell in him, and work holiness in him? The greatness of the blessing lifts it high above the range of merit, and we see that if the Holy Ghost be bestowed, it must be by an act of divine grace—grace infinite in bounty, exceeding all that we could have imagined. "Sovereign grace o'er sin abounding" is here seen in clearest light. "I will put my spirit within you" is a promise which drops with graces as the honeycomb with honey. Listen to the divine music which pours from this word of love. I hear the soft melody of grace, grace, grace, and nothing else but grace. Glory be to God, who gives to sinners the indwelling of his Spirit.

Note, next, that *it is a divine word*: "I will put my spirit within you." Who but the Lord could speak after this fashion? Can one man put the Spirit of God within another? Could all the church combined breathe the Spirit of God into a single sinner's heart? To put any good thing into the deceitful heart of man is a great achievement; but to put the Spirit of God into the heart, truly this is the finger of God. Nay, here I may say, the Lord has made bare his arm, and displayed the fullness of his mighty power. To put the Spirit of God into our nature is a work peculiar to the Godhead, and to do this within the nature of a free agent, such as man, is marvelous. Who but Jehovah, the God of Israel, can speak after this royal style, and, beyond all dispute, declare, "I will put my spirit within you." Men must always surround their resolves with conditions and uncertainties; but since omnipotence is at the back of every promise of God, he speaks like a king; yea, in a style which is only fit for the eternal God. He purposes and promises, and he as surely performs. Sure, then, is this sacred saying, "I will put my spirit within you." Sure, because divine. O sinner, if we poor creatures had the saving of you, we should break down in the attempt; but, behold, the Lord himself comes on the scene, and the work is done! All difficulties are removed by this one sentence, "I will put my spirit within you." We have wrought with our spirit, we have wept over you, and we have entreated you; but we have failed. Lo, there cometh one into the matter who will not fail, with whom nothing is impossible; and he begins his work by saying, "I will put my spirit within you." The word is of grace and of God; regard it, then as a pledge from God of grace.

To me there is much charm in further thought that *this is an individual and personal word*. The Lord means, "I will put my spirit within you": that is to say, within *you*, as individuals. "I will put my spirit within you" one by one. This must be so, since connection requires it. We read in verse 26, "A new heart also will I give you." Now, a new heart can only be given to one person. Each man needs a heart of his own, and each man must have a new heart for himself. "And a new spirit will I put within you." Within each one this must be done. "And I will take away the stony heart out of your flesh, and I will give you an heart of flesh"—these are all personal, individual operations of grace. God deals with men one by one in solemn matters of eternity, sin, and salvation. We are born one by one, and we die one by one: even so we must be born again one by one, and each one for himself must receive Spirit of God. Without this a man has nothing. He cannot be caused to walk in God's statutes except by the infusion of grace into him as an individual. I think I see among my hearers a lone man, or woman, who feels himself, or herself, to be all alone in world, and therefore hopeless. You can believe that God will do great things for a nation, but how shall the solitary be thought of? You are an odd person, one that could not be written down in any list; a peculiar sinner, with constitutional tendencies all your own. Thus saith God, "I will put my spirit within *you*"; within *your* heart—even *yours*. My dear hearers, you who have long been seeking salvation, but have not known power of Spirit—this is what you need. You have been striving in energy of flesh, but you have not understood where your true strength lieth. God saith to you, "Not by might, nor by power, but by my Spirit, saith the Lord"; and again, "I will put my spirit within you." Oh, that this word might be spoken of the Lord to that young man who is ready to despair; to that sorrowful woman who has been looking into herself for power to pray and believe! You are without strength or hope in and of yourself; but this meets your case in all points. "I will put my spirit within you"—within *you* as an individual. Enquire of the Lord for it. Lift up your heart in prayer to God, and ask him to pour upon you the Spirit of grace and of supplications. Plead with the Lord, saying, "Let thy good

Spirit lead me. Even me." Cry, "Pass me not, my gracious Father; but in me fulfill this wondrous word of thine, 'I will put my spirit within you.'"

Note, next, that *this is a separating word*. I do not know whether you will see this readily; but it must be so: this word separates a man from his fellows. Men by nature are of another spirit from that of God, and are under subjection to that evil spirit, the Prince of the power of the air. When the Lord comes to gather out his own, fetching them out from among the heathen, he effects separation by doing according to this word, "I will put my spirit within you." This done, the individual becomes a new man. Those who have the Spirit are not of the world, nor like the world; and soon have to come out from among the ungodly, and to be separate; for [the] difference of nature creates conflict. God's Spirit will not dwell with the evil spirit: you cannot have fellowship with Christ and with Belial; with the kingdom of Heaven and with this world. I wish that the people of God would again wake up to the truth that to gather out a people from among men is the great purpose of the present dispensation. It is still true, as James said at the Jerusalem Council, "Simeon hath declared how God at first did visit the Gentiles, to take out of them a people for his name." We are not to remain clinging to the old wreck with the expectation that we shall pump water out of her and get her safe into port. No; the cry is very different—"Take to the lifeboat! Take to the lifeboat!" You are to quit the wreck, and you are to carry away from the sinking mass that which God will save. You must be separate from the old wreck, lest it suck you down to sure destruction. Your only hope of doing good to the world is by yourselves being "not of the world," even as Christ was not of the world. For you to go down to the world's level will neither be good for it nor for you. That which happened in the days of Noah will be repeated; for when the sons of God entered into alliance with the daughters of men, and there was a league between the two races, the Lord could not endure the evil mixture, but drew up the sluices of the lower deep and swept the earth with a destroying flood. Surely, in that last day of destruction, when the world is overwhelmed with fire, it will be because the church of God shall have degenerated, and the distinctions between the righteous and the wicked shall have been broken down.

The Spirit of God, wherever he comes, doth speedily make and reveal the difference between Israel and Egypt; and in proportion as his active energy is felt, there will be an ever-widening gulf between those who are led of the Spirit and those who are under the dominion of the flesh. The possession of the Spirit will make you, my hearer, quite another sort of man from what you now are, and then you will be actuated by motives which the world will not appreciate; for the world knoweth us not, because it knew him not. Then you will act, and speak, and think, and feel in such a way, that this evil world will misunderstand and condemn you. Since the carnal mind knoweth not the things that are of God—for those things are spiritually discerned—it will not approve your objects and designs. Do not expect it to be your friend. The Spirit which makes you to be of the seed of the woman is not the spirit of the world. The seed of the serpent will hiss at you, and bruise your heel. Your Master said, "Because ye are not of the world, but I have chosen you out of the world; therefore the world hateth you." It is a separating word, this. Has it separated you? Has the Holy Spirit called you alone and blessed you? Do you differ from your old companions? Have you a life they do not understand? If not, may God in mercy put into you that most heavenly deposit, of which he speaks in our; text: "I will put my spirit within you"!

But now notice, that *it is a very uniting word*. It separates from the world, but it joins to God. Note how it runs: "I will put *my* Spirit within *you*." It is not merely *a* spirit, or *the* spirit, but *my* spirit. Now when God's own Spirit comes to reside within our mortal bodies, how near akin we are to the Most High! "Know ye not that your body is the temple of the Holy Ghost?" Does not this make a man sublime? Have you never stood in awe of your own selves, O ye believers? Have you enough regarded even this poor body, as being sanctified and dedicated, and elevated into a sacred condition, by being set apart to be the temple of the Holy Ghost? Thus are we brought into the closest union with God that we can well conceive of. Thus is the Lord our light and our life; while our spirit is subordinated to the divine Spirit. "I will put my spirit within you"—then God himself dwelleth in you. The Spirit of him that raised up Christ from the dead is in you. With Christ, in God your life is hid, and the Spirit seals you, anoints you, and abides in you. By the Spirit we have access to the Father; by the Spirit we perceive our adoption, and learn to cry, "Abba, Father"; by the Spirit we are made partakers of the divine nature, and have communion with the thrice holy Lord.

I cannot help adding here that *it is a very condescending word*—"I will put my spirit within you." Is it really so, that the Spirit of God who displays the power and energetic force of God, by whom God's Word is carried into effect—that the Spirit who of old moved upon the face of the waters, and brought order and life from chaos and death—can it be so that he will deign to sojourn in men? "God in our nature" is a very wonderful conception! God in the babe at Bethlehem, God in the carpenter of Nazareth, God in the "man of sorrows," God in the Crucified, God in him who was buried in the tomb—this is all marvelous. The incarnation is an infinite mystery of love; but we believe it. Yet, if it were possible to compare one illimitable wonder with another, I should say that God's dwelling in his people, and that repeated ten thousand times over, is more marvelous.

That the Holy Ghost should dwell in millions of redeemed men and women, is a miracle not surpassed by that of our Lord's espousal of human nature. For our Lord's body was perfectly pure, and the Godhead, while it dwells with his holy manhood, does at least dwell with a perfect and sinless nature; but the Holy Spirit bows himself to dwell in sinful men; to dwell in men who, after their conversion, still find the flesh warring against the spirit, and the spirit against the flesh; men who are not perfect, though they strive to be so, men who have to lament their shortcomings, and even to confess with shame a measure of unbelief. "I will put my spirit within you" means the abiding of the Holy Spirit in our imperfect nature.

Wonder of wonders! Yet is it as surely a fact as it is a wonder. Believers in the Lord Jesus Christ, you have the Spirit of God, for "if any man have not the Spirit of Christ, he is none of his." You could not bear the suspicion that you are not his; and therefore, as surely as you are Christ's, you have his Spirit abiding in you. The Savior has gone away on purpose that the Comforter might be given to dwell in you, and he does dwell in you. Is it not so? If it be so, admire this condescending God, and worship and praise his name. Sweetly submit to his rule in all things. Grieve not the Spirit of God. Watch carefully that nothing comes within you that may defile the temple of God. Let the faintest monition [warning] of the Holy Spirit be law to you. It was a holy mystery that the presence of the Lord was specially within the veil of the Tabernacle, and that the Lord God spake by Urim and Thummim to his people; it is an equally sacred marvel that now the Holy Ghost dwells in our spirits and abides within our nature and speaks to us whatsoever he hears of the Father. By divine impressions which the opened ear can apprehend, and the tender heart can receive, he speaketh still. God grant us to know his still small voice so as to listen to it with reverent humility and loving joy: then shall we know the meaning of these words, "I will put my spirit within you "

Nor have I yet done with commending my text, for I must not fail to remind you that *it is a very spiritual word.* "I will put my spirit within you" has nothing to do with our wearing a peculiar garb—that would be a matter of little worth. It has nothing to do with affectations of speech—those might readily become a deceptive peculiarity. Our text has nothing to do with outward rites and ceremonies; but goes much further and deeper. It is an instructive symbol when the Lord teaches us our death with Christ by burial in baptism: it is to our great profit that he ordains bread and wine to be tokens of our communion in the body and blood of his dear Son; but these are only outward things, and if they are unattended with the Holy Spirit, they fail of their design. There is something infinitely greater in this promise—"I will put my spirit within you." I cannot give you the whole force of the Hebrew, as to the words "within you," unless I paraphrase them a little, and read "I will put my spirit in the midst of you." The sacred deposit is put deep down in our life's secret place. God puts his Spirit not upon the surface of the man, but into the center of his being. The promise means—"I will put my spirit in your bowels, in your hearts, in the very soul of you." This is an intensely spiritual matter, without admixture [mingling] of anything material and visible. It is spiritual, you see, because it is the Spirit that is given; and he is given internally within our spirit. It is true the Spirit operates upon the external life, but it is through the secret and internal life, and of that inward operation our text speaks. This is what we so greatly require. Do you know what it is to attend a service and hear God's truth faithfully preached, and yet you are forced to say, "Somehow or other it did not enter into me; I did not feel the unction and taste the savor of it"? "I will put my spirit within you," is what you need. Do you not read your Bibles, and even pray, and do not both devotional exercises become too much external acts? "I will put my spirit *within* you" meets this evil. The good Spirit fires your heart; he penetrates your mind; he saturates your soul; he touches the secret and vital springs of your existence. Blessed Word! I love my text. I love it better than I can speak of it.

Observe once more that *this Word is a very effectual one.* "I will put my spirit within you, and cause you to walk in my statutes, and ye shall keep my judgments and do them." The Spirit is operative—first upon the inner life, in causing you to love the law of the Lord; and then it moves you openly to keep his statutes concerning himself, and his judgments between you and your fellow-men. Obedience, if a man should be flogged to it, would be of little worth; but obedience springing out of a life within, this is a priceless breastplate of jewels. If you have a lantern, you cannot make it shine by polishing the glass outside, you must put a candle within it: and this is what God does—he puts the light of the Spirit within us, and then our light shines. He puts his Spirit so deep down into the heart, that the whole nature feels it: it works upward, like a spring from the bottom of a well. It is, moreover, so deeply implanted that there is no removing it. If it were in the memory, you might forget it; if it were in the intellect, you might err in it; but "within you" it touches the whole man, and has dominion over you without fear of failure. When the very kernel of your nature is quickened into holiness, practical godliness is effectually secured. Blessed is he who knows by experience our Lord's words—"The water that I shall give him shall be in him a well of water springing up into everlasting life."

If I should fail in expounding the text, I hope I have so fully commended it to you, that you will turn it over and meditate upon it yourselves, and so get a home-born exposition of it. The key of the text is within its own self; for if the Lord gives you the Spirit, you will then understand his words—"I will put my spirit within you."

II. But now I must work upon *the exposition of the text.*

I trust the Holy Spirit will aid me therein. Let me show you how the good Spirit manifests the fact that he dwells in men. I have to be very brief on a theme that might require a great length of time; and can only mention a part of his ways and workings.

One of the first effects of the Spirit of God being put within us is *quickening*. We are dead by nature to all heavenly and spiritual things; but when the Spirit of God comes, then we begin to live. The man visited of the Spirit begins to feel; the terrors of God make him tremble, the love of Christ makes him weep. He begins to fear, and he begins to hope: a great deal of the first and a very little of the second, it may be. He learns spiritually to sorrow: he is grieved that he has sinned, and that he cannot cease from sinning. He begins to desire that which once he despised: he specially desires to find the way of pardon, and reconciliation with God. Ah, dear hearers! *I* cannot make you feel, *I* cannot make you sorrow for sin, *I* cannot make you desire eternal life; but it is all done as soon as this is fulfilled by the Lord, "I will put my spirit within you." The quickening Spirit brings life to the dead in trespasses and sins.

This life of the Spirit shows itself by causing the man to pray. The cry is the distinctive mark of the living child. He begins to cry, in broken accents, "God be merciful to me." At the same time that he pleads, he feels the soft relentings of repentance. He has a new mind towards sin, and he grieves that he should have grieved his God. With this comes faith; perhaps feeble and trembling, only a touch of the hem of the Savior's robe; but still Jesus is his only hope and his sole trust. To him he looks for pardon and salvation. He dares to believe that Christ can save even him. Then has life come into the soul, when trust in Jesus springs up in the heart.

Remember, dear friends, that as the Holy Spirit gives quickening at the first, so he must revive and strengthen it. Whenever you become dull and faint, cry for the Holy Spirit. Whenever you cannot feel in devotion as you wish to feel, and are unable to rise to any heights of communion with God, plead my text in faith, and beg the Lord to do as he hath said, namely, "I will put my spirit within you." Go to God with this covenant clause, even if you have to confess, "Lord, I am like a log, I am a helpless lump of weakness. Unless thou come and quicken me, I cannot live to thee." Plead importunately [naggingly] the promise, "I will put my spirit within you." All the life of the flesh will [en]gender corruption; all the energy that comes of mere excitement will die down into the black ashes of disappointment; the Holy Ghost alone is the life of the regenerated heart. Have you the Spirit? and if you have him within you, have you only a small measure of his life, and do you wish for more? Then go still where you went at first. There is only one river of the water of life: draw from its floods. You will be lively enough, and bright enough, and strong enough, and happy enough when the Holy Spirit is mighty within your soul.

When the Holy Spirit enters, after quickening, he gives *enlightening*. *We* cannot make men see the truth—they are so blind—but when the Lord puts his Spirit within them, their eyes are opened. At first they may see rather hazily; but still they do see. As the light increases, and the eye is strengthened, they see more and more clearly. What a mercy it is to see Christ—to look unto him—and so to be lightened! By the Spirit, souls see things in their reality: they see the actual truth of them, and perceive that they are facts. The Spirit of God illuminates every believer, so that he sees still more marvelous things out of God's law; but this never happens unless the Spirit opens his eyes. The apostle speaks of being brought "out of darkness into his marvelous light"; and it is a marvelous light, indeed, to come to the blind and dead. Marvelous because it reveals truth with clearness. It reveals marvelous things in a marvelous way. If hills and mountains, if rocks and stones were suddenly to be full of eyes, it would be a strange thing in the earth, but not more marvelous than for you and for me, by the illumination of the Holy Spirit, to see spiritual things. When you cannot make people see the truth, do not grow angry with them, but cry, "Lord, put thy Spirit within them." When you get into a puzzle over the Word of the Lord, do not give up in despair, but believingly cry, "Lord, put thy Spirit within me." Here lies the only true light of the soul. Depend upon it, all that you see by any light except the Spirit of God, you do not spiritually see. If you only see intellectually, or rationally, you do not see to salvation. Unless intellect and reason have received heavenly light, you may see, and yet not see; even as Israel of old. Indeed, your boasted clear sight may aggravate your ruin, like that of the Pharisees, of whom our Lord said, "But now ye say, 'We see', therefore your sin remaineth." O Lord, grant us the Spirit within, for our soul's illumination!

The Spirit also works *conviction*. Conviction is more forcible than illumination: it is the setting of a truth before the eye of the soul, so as to make it powerful upon the conscience. I speak to many here who know what conviction means; still I will explain it from my own experience. I knew what sin meant by my reading, and yet I never knew sin in its heinousness and horror, till I found myself bitten by it, as by a fiery serpent, and felt its poison boiling in my veins. When the Holy Ghost made sin to appear sin, then was I overwhelmed with the sight, and I would fain have fled from myself to escape the intolerable vision. A naked sin stripped of all excuse, and set in the light of truth, is a worse sight than to see the devil himself. When I saw sin as an offense against a just and holy God, committed by such a proud and yet insignificant creature as myself, then was I alarmed. Sirs, did you ever see and feel yourselves to be sinners? "Oh, yes," you say, "we are sinners." O sirs, do you mean it? Do you know what it means? Many of you are no more sinners in your own estimation than you are Hottentots.[1] The beggar who exhibits a sham sore knows not disease; if he did he would have enough of it without presences. To kneel down and say, "Lord, have mercy upon us miserable sinners," and then to get up and feel yourself a very decent sort of body, worthy of commendation, is to mock Almighty God. It is by no means a common thing to get hold of a real sinner, one who is truly so in his own esteem; and it is as pleasant as it is rare, for you can bring to the real sinner the real Savior, and he will welcome him. I do not wonder that Hart said:

> *A sinner is a saved thing,*
> *The Holy Ghost hath made him so.*

---

[1] Hottentots: black Africans (offensive).

The point of contact between a sinner and Christ is sin. The Lord Jesus gave himself for our sins; he never gave himself for our righteousnesses. He comes to heal the sick, and the point he looks to is our sickness. When a physician is called in, he has no patience with things apart from his calling. "Tut, tut!" he cries,

> I do not care about your furniture, nor the number of your cows, nor what income tax you pay, nor what politics you admire; I have come to see a sick man about his disease, and if you will not let me deal with it, I will be gone.

When a sinner's corruptions are loathsome to himself, when his guilt is foul in his own nostrils, when he fears the death that will come of it, then it is that he is really convinced by the Holy Spirit; and no one ever knows sin as his own personal ruin till the Holy Spirit shows it to him. Conviction as to the Lord Jesus comes in the same way. We do not know Christ as our Savior till the Holy Spirit is put within us. Our Lord says, "He shall receive of mine, and shall shew it unto you," and you never see the things of the Lord Jesus till the Holy Ghost shows them to you. To know Jesus Christ as your Savior, as one who died *for you* in particular, is a knowledge which only the Holy Spirit imparts. To apprehend present salvation, as your own personally, comes by your being convinced of it by the Spirit. Oh, to be convinced of righteousness, and convinced of acceptance in the Beloved! This conviction cometh only of him that hath called you, even of him of whom the Lord saith, "I will put my Spirit within you."

Furthermore, the Holy Spirit comes into us for *purification*. "I will put my spirit within you, and cause you to walk in my statutes, and ye shall keep my judgments, and do them." When the Spirit comes, he infuses a new life, and that new life is a fountain of holiness. The new nature cannot sin, because it is born of God, and "it is a living and incorruptible seed." This life produces good fruit, and good fruit only. The Holy Ghost is the life of holiness. At the same time, the coming of the Holy Ghost into the soul gives a mortal stab to the power of sin. The old man is not absolutely dead, but it is crucified with Christ. It is under sentence, and before the eye of the law it is dead; but as a man nailed to a cross may linger long, but yet he cannot live, so the power of evil dies hard, but die it must. Sin is an executed criminal: those nails which fasten it to the cross will hold it fast till no breath remains in it. God the Holy Ghost gives the power of sin its death wound. The old nature struggles in its dying agonies, but it is doomed, and die it must. But you never will overcome sin by your own power, nor by any energy short of that of the Holy Spirit. Resolves may bind it, as Samson was bound with cords; but sin will snap the cords asunder. The Holy Spirit lays the axe at the root of sin, and fall it must. The Holy Ghost within a man is "the Spirit of judgment, the Spirit of burning." Do you know him in that character? As the Spirit of judgment, the Holy Spirit pronounces sentence on sin, and it goes out with the brand of Cain upon it. He does more: he delivers sin over to burning. He executes the death penalty on that which he has judged. How many of our sins have we had to burn alive! And it has cost us no small pain to do it. Sin must be got out of us by fire, if no gentler means will serve; and the Spirit of God is a consuming fire. Truly, "our God is a consuming fire." They paraphrase it, "God, out of Christ, is a consuming fire"; but that is not Scripture. It is "*our* God," our covenant God, who is a consuming fire to refine us from sin. Has not the Lord said, "I will purely purge away all thy dross, and take away all thy sin"? This is what the Spirit does, and it is by no means easy work for the flesh, which would spare many a flattering sin if it could.

The Holy Spirit bedews the soul with purity till he saturates it. Oh, to have a heart saturated with holy influences till it shall be as Gideon's fleece, which held so much dew that Gideon could wring out a bowl full from it! Oh, that our whole nature were filled with the Spirit of God; that we were sanctified wholly—body, soul, and spirit! Sanctification is the result of the Holy Spirit being put within us.

Next, the Holy Ghost acts in the heart as the Spirit of *preservation*. Where he dwells, men do not go back unto perdition. He works in them a watchfulness against temptation day by day. He works in them to wrestle against sin. Rather than sin, a believer would die ten thousand deaths. He works [creates] in believers, union to Christ, which is the source and guarantee of acceptable fruitfulness. He creates in the saints those holy things which glorify God and bless the sons of men. All true fruit is the fruit of the Spirit. Every true prayer must be "praying in the Holy Ghost." He helpeth our infirmities in prayer. Even the hearing of the Word of the Lord is of the Spirit, for John says, "I was in the Spirit on the Lord's day, and heard behind me a great voice." Everything that comes of the man, or is kept alive in the man, is first infused and then sustained and perfected of the Spirit. "It is the spirit that quickeneth; the flesh profiteth nothing." We never go an inch towards Heaven in any other power than that of the Holy Ghost. We do not even stand fast and remain steadfast, except as we are upheld by the Holy Spirit. The vineyard which the Lord hath planted, he also preserves; as it is written, "I, the Lord, do keep it; I will water it every moment; lest any hurt it, I will keep it night and day." Did I hear that young man say, "I should like to become a Christian, but I fear I should not hold out. How am I to be preserved?" [This is] a very proper inquiry, for "He that endureth to the end, the same shall be saved." Temporary Christians are no Christians: only the believer who continues to believe will enter heaven. How, then, can we hold on in such a world as this? Here is the answer. "I will put my spirit within you." When a city has been captured in war, those who formerly possessed it seek to win it back again, but the king who captured it sends a garrison to live within the walls, and he says to the captain, "Take care of this city that I have conquered, and let not the enemy take it again." So the Holy Ghost is the garrison of God within our redeemed humanity, and he will keep us to the end. "May the peace of God, which passeth all understanding, keep your hearts and minds through Christ Jesus." For preservation, then, we look to the Holy Spirit.

Lest I weary you, I will be very brief upon the next point: the Holy Spirit within us is for *guidance*. The Holy Spirit is given to lead us into all truth. Truth is like a vast grotto, and the Holy Spirit brings torches and shows us all the splendor of the roof; and since the passages seem intricate, he knows the way, and he leads us into the deep things of God. He opens up to us one truth after another, by his light and by his guidance, and thus we are "taught of the Lord." He is also our practical guide to heaven, helping and directing us on the upward journey. I wish Christian people oftener inquired of the Holy Ghost as to guidance in their daily life. Know ye not that the Spirit of God dwelleth in you? You need not always be running to this friend and to that to get direction; wait upon the Lord in silence, sit still in quiet before the oracle of God. Use the judgment God has given you; but when that suffices not, resort to him whom Mr. Bunyan calls "the Lord High Secretary," who lives within, who is infinitely wise, and who can guide you by making you to "hear a voice behind you saying, 'This is the way, walk ye in it.'" The Holy Ghost will guide you in life, he will guide you in death, and he will guide you to glory. He will guard you from modern error and from ancient error too. He will guide you in a way that you know not; and through the darkness he will lead you in a way you have not seen. These things will he do unto you, and not forsake you.

Oh, this precious text! I seem to have before me a great cabinet full of jewels rich and rare. May God the Holy Ghost himself come and hand these out to you, and may you be adorned with them all the days of your life!

Last of all, "I will put my spirit within you," that is, by way of *consolation*, for his choice name is "The Comforter." Our God would not have his children unhappy, and therefore he himself, in the third Person of the blessed Trinity, has undertaken the office of Comforter. Why does your face such mournful colors wear? God can comfort you. You that are under the burden of sin; it is true no man can help you into peace, but the Holy Ghost can. O God, to every seeker here who has failed to find rest, grant thy Holy Spirit! Put thy Spirit within him, and he will rest in Jesus. And you, dear people of God, who are worried, remember that worry and the Holy Ghost are very contradictory one to another. "I will put my spirit within you" means that you shall become gentle, peaceful, resigned, and acquiescent in the divine will. Then you will have faith in God that all is well. That text with which I began my prayer this morning was brought home to my heart this week. Our dearly beloved friend Adolph Saphir passed away last Saturday, and his wife died three or four days before him. When my dear brother, Dr. Sinclair

Patteson, went to see him, the beloved Saphir said to him, "God is light, and in him is no darkness at all." Nobody would have quoted that passage but Saphir, the biblical student, the lover of the word, the lover of the God of Israel. "God is light, and in him is no darkness at all." His dear wife is gone, and he himself is ill; but "God is light, and in him is no darkness at all." This is a deep well of overflowing comfort, if you understand it well. God's providence is [his] light as well as his promise, and the Holy Spirit makes us know this. God's word and will and way are all light to his people, and in him is no darkness at all for them. God himself is purely and only light. What if there be darkness in me? There is no darkness in him, and his Spirit causes me to fly to him! What if there be darkness in my family? There is no darkness in my covenant God, and his Spirit makes me rest in him. What if there be darkness in my body by reason of my failing strength? There is no failing in him, and there is no darkness in him—his Spirit assures me of this. David says, "God my exceeding joy"—and such he is to us. "Yea, mine own God is he!" Can you say, "My God, my God"? Do you want anything more? Can you conceive of anything beyond your God? Omnipotent to work all forever! Infinite to give! Faithful to remember! He is all that is good. Light only—"in him is no darkness at all." I have all light, yea, all things, when I have my God. The Holy Spirit makes us apprehend this when he is put within us. Holy Comforter, abide with us, for then we enjoy the light of heaven. Then are we always peaceful and even joyful, for we walk in unclouded light. In him our happiness sometimes rises into great waves of delight, as if it leaped up to the glory. The Lord make this text your own:"I will put my Spirit within you." Amen.

Honey in the Mouth!

A sermon intended for reading on Lord's Day, July 19, 1891, at the conference of the Pastors' College Evangelical Association. No. 2213.

He shall glorify me: for he shall receive of mine, and shall shew it unto you. All things that the Father hath are mine: therefore said I, that he shall take of mine, and shall shew it unto you.—John 16:14–15

Beloved friends, here you have the Trinity, and there is no salvation apart from the Trinity. It must be the Father, the Son, and the Holy Ghost. "All things that the Father hath are mine," saith Christ, and the Father hath all things. They were always his; they are still his; they always will be his; and they cannot become ours till they change ownership, till Christ can say, "All things that the Father hath are mine"; for it is by virtue of the representative character of Christ, standing as the surety of the covenant, that the "all things" of the Father are passed over to the Son, that they might be passed over to us. "It pleased the Father that in him should all fullness dwell; and of his fullness have all we received." But yet we are so dull that, though the conduit-pipe is laid on to the great fountain, we cannot get at it. We are lame; we cannot reach thereto; and in comes the third Person of the divine unity, even the Holy Spirit, and he receives of the things of Christ, and then delivers them over to us. So we do actually receive, through Jesus Christ, by the Spirit, what is in the Father.

Ralph Erskine,[1] in his preface to a sermon upon the fifteenth verse [of this chapter of John], has a notable piece. He speaks of grace as honey—honey for the cheering of the saints, for the sweetening of their mouths and hearts; but he says that in the Father "the honey is in the flower, which is at such a distance from us that we could never extract it." In the Son,

> the honey is in the comb, prepared for us in our Immanuel, God-Man, Redeemer, the Word that was made flesh, saying, "All things that the Father hath are mine; and mine for your use and behoof [benefit]": it is in the comb. But then, next, we have honey in the mouth; the Spirit taking all things, and making application thereof, by showing them unto us, and making us to eat and drink with Christ, and share of these "all things"; yea, not only eat the honey, but the honeycomb with the honey; not only his benefits, but himself.

It is a very beautiful division of the subject. Honey in the flower in God, as in mystery; really there. There never will be any more honey than there is in the flower. There it is. But how shall you and I get at it? We have not wisdom to extract the sweetness. We are not as the bees that are able to find it out. It is bee-honey, but not man-honey. Yet you see in Christ it becomes the honey in the honeycomb, and hence he is sweet to our taste as honey dropping from the comb. Sometimes we are so faint that we cannot reach out a hand to grasp that honeycomb; and, alas! there was a time when our palates were so depraved that we preferred bitter things, and thought them sweet. But now the Holy Ghost has come, we have got the honey in the mouth, and the taste that enjoys it; yea, we have now so long enjoyed it, that the honey of grace has entered into our constitution, and we have become sweet unto God; his sweetness having been conveyed by this strange method unto us.

Beloved friends, I scarcely need say to you, do keep the existence of the Trinity prominent in your ministry. Remember, you cannot pray without the Trinity. If the full work of salvation requires a Trinity, so does that very breath by which we live. You cannot draw near to the Father except through the Son, and by the Holy Spirit. There is a trinity in nature undoubtedly. There certainly constantly turns up the need of a Trinity in the realm of grace; and when we get to Heaven we shall understand, perhaps, more fully what is meant by the Trinity in unity. But if that is a thing never to be understood, we shall at least apprehend it more lovingly; and we shall rejoice more completely as the three tones of our music shall rise up in perfect harmony unto Him who is one and indivisible, and yet is three, forever blessed, Father, Son, and Holy Ghost, one God.

Now, for the point which I am to open up to you this morning; though *I* cannot do it, but *he* must do it. We must sit here, and have the text acted out upon

---

[1] Ralph Erskine: Scottish clergyman, 1685-1752.

ourselves. "He shall glorify me. He shall take of mine, and shall shew it unto you." May it be so just now!

First, *what the Holy Spirit does*: "He shall take of mine, and shall shew it unto you." Secondly, *what the Holy Spirit aims at and really effects*: "He shall glorify me." And then, thirdly, *how in doing both these things he is the Comforter*. It is the Comforter that does this; and we shall find our richest, surest comfort in this work of the Holy Spirit, who shall take of the things of Christ, and show them unto us.

I. First, *what the Holy Spirit does*.

It is clear, beloved friends, that the Holy Spirit *deals with the things of Christ*. As our brother, Archibald Brown, said, when expounding the chapter just now, he [the Holy Spirit] does not aim at any originality. He deals with the things of Christ. All things that Christ had heard from his Father, he made known to us. He kept to them. And now the Spirit takes of the things of Christ, and of nothing else. Do not let us strain at anything new. The Holy Ghost could deal with anything in Heaven above, or in the earth beneath—the story of the ages past, the story of the ages to come, the inward secrets of the earth, the evolution of all things, if there be an evolution. He could do it all. Like the Master, he could handle any topic he chose; but he confines himself to the things of Christ, and therein finds unutterable liberty and boundless freedom.

Do you think, dear friend, that you can be wiser than the Holy Spirit? And if his choice must be a wise one, will yours be a wise one if you begin to take of the things of something or somebody else? You will have the Holy Spirit near you when you are receiving of the things of Christ; but, as the Holy Spirit is said never to receive anything else, when you are handling other things on the Sabbath-day, you will be handling them alone; and the pulpit is a dreary solitude, even in the midst of a crowd, if the Holy Ghost is not with you there. You may, if you please, excogitate [develop] a theology out of your own vast brain; but the Holy Ghost is not with you there. And, mark you! there are some of us that are resolved to tarry with the things of Christ, and keep on dealing with them as far as he enables us to do so; and we feel that we are in such blessed company with the divine Spirit, that we do not envy you that wider range of thought, if you prefer it.

The Holy Spirit still exists, and works, and teaches in the church; but we have a test by which to know whether what people claim to be revelation, is revelation or not: "He shall receive of mine." The Holy Ghost will never go farther than the cross and the coming of the Lord. He will go no farther than that which concerns Christ. "He shall receive of mine." When, therefore, anybody whispers in my ear that there has been revealed to him this or that, which I do not find in the teaching of Christ and his apostles, I tell him that we must be taught by the Holy Spirit. His one vocation is to deal with the things of Christ. If we do not remember this, we may be carried away by vagaries, as many have been. Those who will have to do with other things, let them; but as for us, we shall be satisfied to confine our thoughts and our teaching within these limitless limits: "He shall take of mine, and shall shew it unto you."

I like to think of the Holy Spirit handling such things. They seem so worthy of him. Now has he got among the hills. Now is his mighty mind among the infinities when he has to deal with Christ, for Christ is the Infinite veiled in the finite. Why, he seems something *more* than infinite when he gets into the finite; and the Christ of Bethlehem is less to be understood than the Christ of the Father's bosom. He seems, if it were possible, to have out-infinited the infinite, and the Spirit of God has themes here worthy of his vast nature.

When you have been the whole Sunday morning whittling away a text to the small end of nothing, what have you done? A king spent a day in trying to make a portrait on a cherry-stone—a king, who was ruling empires; and here is a minister, who professes to have been called of the Holy Ghost to the employ of taking of the things of Christ, who spent a whole morning with precious souls, who were dying while he spoke to them, in handling a theme, concerning which it did not signify the turn of a hair whether it was so or not. Oh, imitate the Holy Spirit! If you profess to have him dwelling in you, be moved by him. Let it be said of you in your measure, as of the Holy Ghost without measure, "He shall receive of mine, and shall shew it unto you."

But, next, what does the Holy Ghost do? Why, *he deals with feeble men*, yea, he dwells with us poor creatures. I can understand the Holy Ghost taking the things of Christ, and rejoicing therein; but the marvel is, that he should glorify Christ by coming and showing these things to us. And yet, brethren, it is among us that Christ is to get his glory. Our eyes must see him. An unseen Christ is little glorious; and the things of Christ unknown, the things of Christ untasted and unloved, seem to have lost their brilliance to a high degree. The Holy Spirit, therefore—feeling that to show a sinner the salvation of Christ glorifies him—spends his time, and has been spending these centuries, in taking of the things of Christ, and showing them to us. Ah! it is a great condescension on his part to show them to us; but it is a miracle, too. If it were reported that suddenly stones had life, and hills had eyes, and trees had ears, it would be a strange thing; but for us who were dead and blind and deaf in an awful sense—for the spiritual is more emphatic than the natural—for us to be so far gone, and for the Holy Ghost to be able to show the things of Christ to us, is to his honor. But he *does* do it. He comes from Heaven to dwell with us. Let us honor and bless his name.

I never could make up my mind which to admire most as an act of condescension; the incarnation of Christ, or the indwelling of the Holy Ghost. The incarnation of Christ is marvelous—that he should dwell in human nature; but, observe, the Holy Ghost dwells in human nature in its sinfulness; not in perfect human nature, but in imperfect human nature; and he continues to dwell, not in one body, which was fashioned strangely for himself, and was pure and without taint; but he dwells in *our* body. Know ye not that they are the temples of the Holy Ghost, which were defiled by nature, and in which a measure of defilement still remains, despite his indwelling? And this he has done these multitudes of years, not in one instance, nor in thousands of instances only, but in a number that no man can number. He continues still to come into contact with sinful humanity. Not to the angels, nor to the seraphim, nor to the cherubim, nor to the host who have washed their robes, and made them white in the blood of the Lamb, does he show the things of Christ; but he shall show them unto *us*.

I suppose that it means this, that *he takes of [all] the words of our Lord*—those which he spoke personally, *and* by his apostles. Let us never allow anybody to divide between the word of the apostles and the word of Christ. Our Savior has joined them together. "Neither pray I for these alone, but for them also which shall believe on me through their word." And if any begin rejecting the apostolic word, they will be outside the number for whom Christ prays; they shut themselves out by that very fact. I wish that they would solemnly recollect that the word of the apostles is the word of Christ. He tarried not long enough, after he had risen from the dead, to give us a further exposition of his mind and will; and he could not have given it before his death, because it would have been unsuitable. "I have yet many things to say unto you, but ye cannot bear them now." After the descent of the Holy Ghost, the disciples were prepared to receive that which Christ spoke by his servants Paul and Peter, and James and John. Certain doctrines which we are sometimes taunted about, as being not revealed by Christ, but by his apostles, were all revealed by Christ, everyone of them. They can all be found in his teaching; but they are very much in the parabolic [parable] form. It is after he has gone up into glory, and has prepared a people by his Spirit to understand the truth more fully, that he sends his apostles, and says, "Go forth, and open up to those whom I have chosen out of the world, the meaning of all I said." The meaning is all there, just as all the New Testament is in the Old; and sometimes I have thought that, instead of the Old being less inspired than the New, it is more inspired. Things are packed away more tightly in the Old Testament than in the New, if possible. There are worlds of meaning in one pregnant line in the Old Testament; and in Christ's words it is just so. He is the Old Testament to which the Epistles come in as a kind of New Testament; but they are all one and indivisible; they cannot be separated.

Well, now, the words of the Lord Jesus, and the words of his apostles, are to be *expounded* to us by the Holy Spirit. We shall never get at the center of their meaning apart from his teaching. We shall never get at their meaning at all, if we begin disputing about the words, saying, "Now, I cannot accept the words." If you will not have the shell, you will never have the chick. It is impossible. "The words are not inspired," they say. Here is a man in the witness-box, and he has sworn to speak the truth, and he says that he has done so; and now he is cross-examined, and he says, "Now, I have spoken the truth, but I do not stand by my words." The cross-examining lawyer has got hold of a certain statement of his. The witness says, "Oh, I do not swear to the words, you know." The question is asked, "What, then, do you swear to? There is nothing else. We do not know anything about your meaning. All that you have sworn to must be your words." But what the fellow means is this, that he is a liar; he is a perjurer. Well, I say no more than common-sense would suggest to you if you were sitting in a court. Now, if a man says, "I have spoken the truth, but still I do not swear to the words;" what is there left? If we have no inspiration in the words, we have got an impalpable inspiration that oozes away between your fingers, and leaves nothing behind.

Well, take the words, and never dispute over them. Still, into their soul-fullness of meaning you cannot come until the Holy Ghost shall lead you into them. They that wrote them for you did not fully understand what they wrote in many instances. There were some of them who enquired and searched diligently to know what manner of things those were, whereof the Holy Ghost had spoken to them, and of which he had made them speak. And you to whom the words come will have to do the same. You must go and say,

> Great Master, we thank thee for the Book with all our hearts; and we thank thee for putting the Book into words; but now, good Master, we will not cavil over the letter, as did the Jews and the rabbis and the scribes of old, and so miss thy meaning. Open wide the door of the words, that we may enter into the secret closet of the meaning; and teach us this, we pray thee. Thou hast the key. Lead us in.

Dear friends, whenever you want to understand a text of Scripture, try to read the original. Consult anybody who has studied what the original means; but remember that the quickest way into a text is praying in the Holy Ghost. Pray the chapter over. I do not hesitate to say that, if a chapter is read upon one's knees, looking up, at every word, to him that gave it, the meaning will come to you with infinitely more light than by any other method of studying it. "He shall glorify me: for he shall receive of mine, and shall shew it unto you." He shall re-deliver the Master's message to you in the fullness of its meaning.

But I do not think that is all that the text means. "He shall receive of mine." In the next verse the Lord goes on to say, "All things that the Father hath are mine." I do think that it means, therefore, *that the Holy Spirit will show us the things of Christ.* Here is a text for us—"The things of Christ." Christ speaks as if he had not any things just then which were specially his own, for he had not died then; he had not risen then; he was not pleading then as the great Intercessor in heaven: all that was to come. But still, he says,

> Even now all things that the Father hath are mine: all his attributes, all his glory, all his rest, all his happiness, all his blessedness. *All that* is mine, and the Holy Ghost shall show that to you.

But I might almost read my text in another light, for he *has* died, and risen, and gone on high, and lo, he cometh. His chariots are on the way. Now, there are certain things which the Father hath, and which Jesus Christ hath, which are truly the things of Christ, emphatically the things of Christ; and my prayer is, that you and I, preachers of the gospel, might have this text fulfilled in us: "He shall take of mine—my things—and shall show them unto you."

Suppose, dear brethren, that we are going to preach the word again, and the Holy Spirit shows to us our Master in his Godhead. Oh, how we will preach him as divine—how surely he can bless our congregation! How certainly he must be able to subdue all things unto himself, seeing that he is very God of very God! It is equally sweet to see him as man. Oh, to have the Spirit's view of Christ's manhood! Distinctly to recognize that he is bone of my bone, and flesh of my flesh, and that in his infinite tenderness he will compassionate me, and deal with my poor people, and with the troubled consciences that are round me; that I have still to go to them, and tell them of One who is touched with the feeling of their infirmities, having been tempted in all points like as they still are! Oh, my brothers, if we once—nay, if *every* time before we preach—we get a view of Christ in his divine and human natures, and come down fresh from that vision to speak about him, what glorious preaching it would be for our people!

It is a glorious thing to get a view of the offices of Christ by the Holy Spirit; but especially of his office as a Savior. I have often said to him,

> You must save my people. It is no business of mine. I never set up in that line [of work], or put over my door that I was a savior; but thou hast been apprenticed to this trade. Thou hast learned it by experience, and thou dost claim it as thine own honor. Thou art exalted on high to be a Prince and a Savior. Do thine own work, my Lord.

I took this text, and used it with sinners the other Sunday night, and I know that God blessed it when I said to them,

> May the Holy Ghost show you that Christ is a Savior! A physician does not expect you to make any apologies when you call upon him because you are ill, for he is a physician, and he wants you in order that he may prove his skill; so Christ is a Savior, and you need not apologize for going to him; because he cannot be a Savior if there is not somebody to be saved.

The fact is, Christ cannot get ahold of us anywhere except by our sin. The point of contact between the sick one and the physician is the disease. Our sin is the point of contact between us and Christ. Oh, that the Spirit of God would take of Christ's divine offices, especially that of a Savior, and show them unto us!

Did the Holy Ghost ever show to you these thing of Christ, namely, his covenant engagements? When he struck [shook] hands with the Father, it was that he would bring many sons unto glory; that of those whom the Father gave him, he would lose none, but that they should be saved; for he is under bonds to his Father to bring his elect home. When the sheep have to pass again under the hand of him that telleth them, they will go under the rod one by one, each one having the blood-mark; and he will never rest till the number in the heavenly fold shall tally with the number in the book. So I believe, and it has seemed delightful to me to have this shown to me when I have gone to preach. It is a dull, dreary, wet, foggy morning. There are only a few present. Yes; but they are picked people, whom God hath ordained to be there, and there will be the right number there. I shall preach, and there will be some saved. We do not go at a peradventure [uncertainty]; but, guided by the blessed Spirit of God, we go with a living certainty, knowing that God has a people that Christ is bound to bring home, and bring them home he will; and while he shall see of the travail of his soul, his Father shall delight in everyone of them. If you get a clear view of that, it will give you backbone and make you strong. "He shall take of mine, and shall show you my covenant engagements, and when you see them you shall be comforted."

But, beloved, the Holy Ghost favors you by taking what is peculiarly Christ's, namely, his love, and showing that to you. We have seen it, seen it sometimes more vividly than at other times. But if the full blaze of the Holy Spirit were to be concentrated upon the love of Christ, and our eyesight enlarged to its utmost capacity, it would be such a vision that Heaven could not excel it. We should sit with our Bible before us in our study, and feel, "Well now, here is a man, whether in the body or out of the body, I cannot tell. Such a man is caught up into the third heaven." Oh, to see the love of Christ in the light of the Holy Ghost! When it is so revealed to us, it is not merely the surface which we see, but the love of Christ itself. You know that you never saw anything yet, strictly speaking. You only see the appearance of the thing—the light reflected by it; that is all you see. But the Holy Ghost shows us the naked truth, the essence of the love of Christ; and what that essence is—that love without beginning, without change, without limit, without end; and that love set upon his people simply from motives within himself, and from no motive *ab extra*—what that must be, what tongue can tell? Oh, it is a ravishing sight!

I think that if there could be one sight more wonderful than the love of Christ, it would be the blood of Christ.

> *Much we talk of Jesu's blood,*
> *But how little's understood.*

It is the climax of God. I do not know of anything more divine. It seems to me as if all the eternal purposes worked up to the blood of the cross, and then worked from the blood of the cross towards the sublime consummation of all things. Oh, to think that he should become man! God has made spirit, pure spirit, embodied spirit; and then materialism; and somehow, as if he would take all up into one, the Godhead links himself with the material, and he wears dust about him even as we wear it; and taking it all up, he then goes, and, in that fashion, redeems his people from all the evil of their soul, their spirit, and their body, by the pouring out of a life which, while it was human, was so in connection with the divine, that we speak correctly of "the blood of God." Turn to the twentieth chapter of the Acts, and read how the apostle Paul puts it: "Feed the church of God, which he hath purchased with his own blood." I believe that Dr. [Isaac] Watts is not wrong when he says—"God that loved and died." It is an incorrect accuracy, a strictly absolute accuracy of incorrectness. So it must be ever when the finite talks of the Infinite. It was a wonderful sacrifice that could absolutely obliterate, annihilate, and extinguish sin, and all the traces that could possibly remain of it; for "He hath finished the transgression, made an end of sins, made reconciliation for iniquity, and brought in everlasting righteousness." Ah, dear friends! You have seen this, have you not? But you have to see more of it yet; and when we get to heaven, we shall then know what that blood means, and with what vigor shall we sing, "Unto him that loved us, and washed us from our sins in his own blood"! Will anybody be there to say, "Is not that the religion of the shambles?" as they blasphemously call it. Ah, my friends! They will find themselves where they will wish they *had* believed "the religion of the shambles"; and I think that it will burn like coals of juniper into the soul of any man that has ever dared to talk like that, that he did despite [contemptuous disregard] unto the blood of God, and so, by his own willful deeds, will be cast away forever.

May the Holy Spirit show unto you Gethsemane, and Gabbatha,[2] and Golgotha! and then, may it please him to give you a sight of what our Lord is now doing! Oh, how it would cheer you up at any time when you were depressed, only to see him standing and pleading for you! Do you not think that if your wife is ill, and your child is sick, and there is scant food in the cupboard; if you were to go out at the back door, and you saw him with the breastplate on, and all the stones glittering, and your name there, and him pleading for you, you would go in and say, "There, wife, it is all right. He is praying for us"? Oh, it would be a comfort if the Holy Ghost showed you a pleading Christ! And then, to think that he is reigning as well as pleading. He, is at the right hand of God, even the Father, who hath put all things under his feet. And he waits till the last enemy shall lie there. Now, you are not afraid, are you, of those who have been snubbing you and opposing you?

---

[2] Gabbatha: The hall where Jesus was judged, John 18–19.

Remember, he hath said, "All power is given unto me in Heaven and in earth. Go ye therefore, and teach all nations; and lo, I am with you alway, even unto the end of the world."

Next, and best of all, may the Holy Spirit give you a clear view of his coming. This is our most brilliant hope: "Lo, he cometh!" The more the adversary waxes bold, and the less of faith there is, and when zeal seems almost extinct—these are the tokens of his coming. The Lord always said so; and that he would not come unless there was a falling away first; and so the darker the night grows, and the fiercer the storm becomes, the better will we remember that he of the lake of Galilee came to them upon the waves in the night when the storm was wildest. Oh, what will his enemies say when he comes? When they behold the nail-prints of the Glorified, and the Man with the thorn Crown—when they see him really come—they that have despised his word, and his ever-blessed blood, how will they flee before that face of injured love! And we, on the contrary, through his infinite mercy, will say, "This is what the Holy Ghost showed us; and now we behold it literally. We thank him for the foresights which he gave us of the beatific vision."

I have not done on the first head yet, because there is one point which I want you to recollect. When the Holy Ghost takes of the things of Christ, and shows them to us, he has a purpose in so doing. You will not laugh, I hope, when I remind you of what the little boys sometimes do at school with one another. I have seen a boy take out of his pocket an apple, and say to his schoolmate, "Do you see that apple?" "Yes," says the other. "Then, you may see me eat it," says he. But the Holy Ghost is no Tantalus, taking of the things of Christ, and holding them up to mock us. No: he says, "Do you see these things? If you can see them, you may have them." Did not Christ himself say, "Look unto me, and be ye saved, all the ends of the earth"? Looking gives you a claim; and if you can see him, he is yours. It is with you, with regard to the Spirit showing you things, as it was with Jacob. You know Jacob lay down, and went to sleep, and the Lord said to him, "The land whereon thou liest, to thee will I give it." Now, wherever you go, throughout the whole of Scripture, if you can find a place where you can lie down, that is yours. If you can sleep on a promise, that promise is yours. "Lift up now thine eyes," said God to Abraham, "and look from the place where thou art northward, and southward, and eastward, and westward: for all the land which thou seest, to thee will I give it." The Lord increase our holy vision of delighted faith; for there is nothing you see, but you may also enjoy; all that is in Christ, is there for you.

II. Now, secondly, *what the Holy Spirit aims at, and what he really accomplishes.* **"He shall glorify me."**

Ah, brothers! The Holy Ghost never comes to glorify *us*, or to glorify a denomination, or, I think, even to glorify a systematic arrangement of doctrines. He comes to glorify Christ. If we want to be in accord with him, we must preach in order to glorify Christ. May we never have this thought—"I will put that bit in; it will tell well. The friends will feel that oratory is not quite extinct, that Demosthenes lives again in this village." No, no. I should say, brother, though it is a very delightful piece, strike that out ruthlessly; because if you have had a thought of that kind about it, you had better not put yourself in the way of temptation by using it.

> Yes, that is a magnificent sentence! I do not know where I met with it, or whether it is my own. I am afraid that most of our friends will not understand it; but then it will give them an impression that they have a deep thinker in their pulpit.

Well then, it may be very admirable, and, further, it might be a very right thing to give them that precious piece; but if you have that thought about it, strike it out. Strike it out ruthlessly. Say,

> No, no, no! If it is not distinctly my aim to glorify Christ, I am not in accord with the aim of the Holy Ghost, and I cannot expect his help. We shall not be pulling the same way, and therefore I will have nothing of which I cannot say that I am saying it simply, sincerely, and only that I may glorify Christ.

How, then, does the Holy Spirit glorify Christ? It is very beautiful to think that he glorifies Christ *by showing Christ's things*. If you wanted to do honor to a man, you would perhaps take him a present to decorate his house. But here, if you want to glorify Christ, you must go and take the things *out* of Christ's house, "the things of Christ." Whenever we have to praise God, what do we do? We simply say what he is. "Thou art this, and thou art that." There is no other praise. We cannot fetch anything from elsewhere, and bring it to God; but the praises of God are simply the facts about himself. If you want to praise the Lord Jesus Christ, tell the people about him. Take of the things of Christ, and show them to the people, and you will glorify Christ. Alas! I know what you will do. You will weave words together, and you will form and fashion them, in a marvelous manner, till you have produced a charming piece of literature. When you have carefully done that, put it in the fire under the oven, and let it burn. Possibly you may help to bake some bread with it. Brethren, it is better for us to tell what Christ is, than to invent ten thousand fine words of praise in reference to him. "He shall glorify me, for he shall receive of mine, and shall shew it unto you."

Again, I think that the blessed Spirit glorifies Christ by showing us the things of Christ *as Christ's*. Oh, to be pardoned! Yes, it is a great thing; but to find that pardon in his wounds, that is a greater thing! Oh, to get peace! Yes, but to find that peace in the blood of his cross! Brethren, have the blood-mark very visibly on all your mercies. They are all marked with the blood of the cross; but sometimes we think so much of the sweetness of the bread, or of the coolness of the waters, that we forget whence these came, and how they came, and then they lack their choicest flavor. That it came from Christ is the best thing about the best thing that ever came from

Christ. That he saves me is, somehow, better than my being saved. It is a blessed thing to go to Heaven; but I do not know that it is not a better thing to be in Christ, and so, as the result of it, to get into heaven. It is himself, and that which comes of himself, that becomes best of all, because it comes of himself. So the Holy Ghost shall glorify Christ by making us see that these things of Christ are indeed of Christ, and completely of Christ, and still are in connection with Christ; and we only enjoy them because we are in connection with Christ.

Then it is said in the text, "He shall glorify me: for he shall take of mine, and shall shew it *unto you*?" Yes, it does glorify Christ for the Holy Spirit to show Christ to us. How often I have wished that men of great minds might be converted! I have wished that we could have a few Miltons, and such like men, to sing of the love of Christ; a few mighty men, who teach politics, and the like, to consecrate their talents to the preaching of the gospel. Why is it not so? Well, because the Holy Ghost does not seem to think that that would be the way to glorify Christ supremely; and he prefers, as a better way, to take us common-place sort of persons, and to take the things of Christ, and to show them to *us*. He does glorify Christ; and blessed be his name, that ever my bleary eyes should look upon his infinite loveliness; that ever such a wretch as I, who can understand everything but what I ought to understand, should be made to comprehend the heights and depths—and to know, with all saints, the love of Christ, that passeth knowledge. You see, in a school, that clever boy. Well, it is not much for the master to have made a scholar of him. But here is one who shines as a scholar, and his mother says that he was the greatest dolt in the family. All his schoolfellows say, "Why, he was our butt! He seemed to have no brains; but our master, somehow, got some brain into him, and made him know something which he appeared, at one time, incapable of knowing." Somehow, it does seem to be as if our very folly, and impotence, and spiritual death—if the Holy Ghost shows to us the things of Christ—will go towards the increase of that great glorifying of Christ at which the Holy Spirit aims.

Then, beloved brethren, since it is for the honor of Christ for his things to be shown to men, he will show them to us, *that we may go and show them to other people*. This we cannot do, except as he is with us to make the others to see; but he will be with us while we tell forth what he has taught us; and so the Holy Ghost will really be showing to others while he is showing to us. A secondary influence will flow from this service, for we shall be helped to *use the right means* to make others see the things of Christ.

III. Our time is almost gone; but in the third place I must just point out to you *how he is in both of these things our comforter.*

He is so, firstly, for this reason—that *there is no comfort in the world like a sight of Christ*. He shows to us the things of Christ. Oh, brethren, if you are poor, and if the

Holy Ghost shows you that Christ had not where to lay his head, what a sight for you! And if you are sick, and if the Holy Ghost shows you what sufferings Christ endured, what comfort comes to you! If you are made to see the things of Christ, each thing according to the condition which you are in, how speedily you are delivered out of your sorrow!

And then, if the Holy Ghost glorifies Christ, *that is the cure for every kind of sorrow*. He is the Comforter. I may have told you before, but I cannot help telling you again, that many years ago, after the terrible accident in the Surrey Gardens, I had to go away into the country, and keep quite still.[3] The very sight of the Bible made me cry. I could only keep alone in the garden; and I was heavy and sad, for people had been killed in the accident; and there I was, half dead myself; and I remember how I got back my comfort, and I preached on the Sabbath after I recovered. I had been walking round the garden, and I was standing under a tree. If it is there now, I should know it: And I remember these words: "Him hath God exalted with his right hand to be a Prince and a Savior." "Oh," I thought to myself, "I am only a common soldier. If I die in a ditch, I do not care. The king is honored. He wins the victory;" and I was like those French soldiers in the old times, who loved the emperor; and you know how, when they were dying, if he rode by, the wounded man would raise himself up on his elbow, and cry once more, *"Vive l'Empereur!"*—for the emperor was graven on his heart. And so, I am sure, it is with every one of you, my comrades, in this holy war. If our Lord and King is exalted, then let other things go which way they like: if he is exalted, never mind what becomes of us. We are a set of pigmies; it is all right if *he* is exalted. God's truth is safe, we are perfectly willing to be forgotten, derided, slandered, or anything else that men please. The cause is safe, and the King is on the throne. Hallelujah! Blessed be his name!

---

[3] "...On Sundays [the Surrey Music Hall] was used temporarily . . . for the religious services held by the late Mr. Spurgeon, on his first rush into popularity; and on the first occasion of holding these services—the evening of October 19, 1856—it was the scene of a serious and fatal accident, seven persons being killed by a false alarm of fire raised by some reckless and wanton jesters." From *Old And New London,* published 1897, as posted on the Internet at www.arthurlloyd.co.uk/Surreyhall.htm.

Index to Key Scriptures

Isaiah 40:6–8	*The Withering Work of the Spirit*	67
Ezekiel 36:27	*The Covenant Promise of the Spirit*	123
Haggai 2:4–5	*The Abiding of the Spirit Is the Glory of the Church*	109
John 3:8	*The Holy Spirit Compared to the Wind*	53
John 7:38–39	*The Indwelling and Outflowing of the Holy Spirit*	95
John 14:26	*The Comforter*	1
John 16:7	*The Indwelling and Outflowing of the Holy Spirit*	95
John 16:13	*The Holy Ghost, the Great Teacher*	27
John 16:14–15	*Honey in the Mouth!*	137
Acts 2:2–4	*The Pentecostal Wind and Fire*	81
Acts 10:44	*The Outpouring of the Holy Spirit*	41
Romans 15:13	*The Power of the Holy Ghost*	13
1 Peter 1:23–25	*The Withering Work of the Spirit*	67